THE MOST AMAZING FACTS FOR CURIOUS MINDS

568 MIND BLOWING FACTS ABOUT THE HUMAN BODY IT ORGANS AND HOW IT WORKS.

By

RAPHAEL ELIOT

TABLE OF CONTENTS

CONCLUSION

INTRODUCTION

Welcome to my Interesting Health Facts", your go-to source for fascinating and surprising insights into the world of health and the human body. Whether you're a health enthusiast or just curious about how your body works, this book offers a fun, light-hearted approach to learning new things about the systems that keep you alive and thriving.

From quirky facts about bones and muscles to jaw-dropping discoveries about the brain and heart, you'll find each page packed with information that's both educational and entertaining. We'll uncover myths, explain the science behind everyday health practices, and dive into the history and future of medicine, all while keeping things easy to understand and engaging.

Did you know that your stomach gets a brand new lining every few days? Or that laughing can actually boost your immune system? Whether you're looking to impress your friends with trivia or just want to know more about the human body, you're in the right place.

BONE FACTS

1: The Framework of Your Body

Our bones are incredible structures that provide support, shape, and protection to our bodies. While they may seem static, bones are actually dynamic, living tissues that constantly grow, break down, and regenerate. Let's explore some fascinating facts about the framework that keeps us moving and upright!

2: Your Skeleton Has 206 Bones

While babies are born with about 270 bones, many of these fuse together as they grow, leaving adults with 206 bones.

3: Bones Are Stronger Than Steel

Ounce for ounce, bone is stronger than steel. A cubic inch of bone can bear the weight of up to five standard pickup trucks!

4: The Femur Is the Longest and Strongest Bone

Your thigh bone, or femur, is the longest and strongest bone in your body. It plays a critical role in supporting your weight and allows you to stand, walk, and jump.

5: Small but Mighty: The Stapes Bone

The smallest bone in your body is the stapes, found in your middle ear. It's less than 3 millimeters long but plays a crucial role in hearing by transmitting sound vibrations.

6: Your Bones Are 60% Water

Although bones are hard and seem dry, they're actually made up of about 60% water. The rest is a mix of collagen, calcium, and other minerals that give bones their strength.

7: Bones Heal Themselves

Unlike many other tissues, bones have the remarkable ability to heal themselves when fractured. Bone cells called osteoblasts create new bone to bridge the gap, though the process can take weeks or even months depending on the injury.

8: You Get a New Skeleton Every 10 Years

Your skeleton completely regenerates itself about every 10 years through a process called bone remodeling.

9: Bone Is a Storage Depot for Minerals

Bones store important minerals like calcium and phosphorus, which are essential for many bodily functions, including nerve transmission and muscle contraction.

10: Your Hands and Feet Contain Over Half of Your Bones

The human hand has 27 bones, and the foot has 26. Together, these bones make up more than half of all the bones in your body!

11: Bones Are Light but Strong

Despite being incredibly strong, bones are surprisingly lightweight. This balance of strength and lightness allows us to move freely without being weighed down

12: Bones Are Alive

Bones may seem like rigid, lifeless structures, but they are very much alive. They contain living cells like osteoblasts, which help form new bone, and osteoclasts, which break down old bone tissue.

13: Babies Have More Bones Than Adults

Babies are born with about 270 bones. As they grow, many of these bones fuse together, which is why adults only have 206. For example, the bones of a baby's skull fuse over time to protect the brain.

14: Bones Are the Lightest Part of Your Body

Despite their strength, bones are actually quite light, which allows us to move easily. Your skeleton accounts for only about 14% of your total body weight!

15: The Human Skull Is Made Up of 22 Bones

The skull is a complex structure that consists of 22 individual bones. These bones are fused together to protect the brain, and the only movable bone in the skull is the jawbone, or mandible.

16: Bone Marrow Produces Blood Cells

Deep inside many of your bones is bone marrow, a soft tissue responsible for producing red blood cells, white blood cells, and platelets. In fact, around 200 billion red blood cells are made each day in the marrow!

17: Hyoid Bone: The Only Floating Bone

The hyoid bone, located in your throat, is the only bone in your body not connected to any other bone. It helps support your tongue and plays a crucial role in speech and swallowing.

18: Bone Density Peaks in Your 30s

Your bones reach their maximum density in your early 30s. After that, bone density begins to decline slowly, which is why maintaining a diet rich in calcium and getting regular exercise is important as you age.

19: Women Are More Prone to Osteoporosis

Due to hormonal changes after menopause, women are more likely to develop osteoporosis, a condition that weakens bones and makes them more susceptible to fractures.

20: The Collarbone Is the Most Commonly Broken Bone

The clavicle, or collarbone, is one of the most commonly broken bones, especially during falls or accidents. Its vulnerable position makes it easy to fracture.

21: Teeth Are Not Technically Bones

While teeth and bones are both hard and contain calcium, teeth are not classified as bones. Teeth are made of dentin and enamel, the latter being the hardest substance in the human body.

22: The Patella: A Unique Bone

Your kneecap, or patella, is a sesamoid bone, meaning it is embedded within a tendon. It acts like a shield for your knee joint, protecting it and enhancing the movement of the muscles around it.

23: Some People Have Extra Bones

While most people have 206 bones, some individuals are born with extra bones, such as additional ribs or bones in the feet called accessory bones. These variations are usually harmless.

24: Your Bones Give You Shape

Bones define the shape of your body, influencing your height, posture, and overall appearance. They work with muscles to provide structure and movement.

25: Bone Infections Are Rare but Serious

Though rare, bones can get infected in a condition called osteomyelitis. This is usually caused by bacteria entering the bone through a wound or surgery and requires prompt treatment.

26: Archaeologists Learn from Bones

Bones can tell scientists a lot about ancient civilizations, including diet, lifestyle, and even certain diseases. Studying bones gives us insight into human history and evolution.

MUSCLE FACTS

27: Facts About Strength and Endurance

Muscles are the engines of the human body, driving everything from the simplest blink of an eye to the most powerful sprint. They come in all shapes and sizes, and their ability to adapt to the demands placed on them is extraordinary. Let's dive into some amazing facts about the strength, endurance, and complexity of our muscles!

28: The Human Body Has Over 600 Muscles

There are more than 600 muscles in your body, making up around 40% of your total body weight. They're responsible for every move you make, from typing on a keyboard to running a marathon.

29: The Strongest Muscle Based on Weight: The Masseter

Pound for pound, the masseter, or jaw muscle, is the strongest muscle in the body. It's responsible for chewing and can exert a force of up to 200 pounds on the molars!

30: The Gluteus Maximus Is the Largest Muscle

The gluteus maximus, or your buttock muscle, is the largest and one of the strongest muscles in the body. It helps with walking, running, and keeping you upright.

31: Muscles Grow Stronger by Tearing

When you exercise, it causes little tears in your muscle filaments. As these tears repair, your muscles grow back thicker and stronger, which is how strength training increases muscle size.

32: The Heart Is the Hardest-Working Muscle

Your heart never stops working, pumping roughly 2,000 gallons of blood through your body every day. Over the course of a lifetime, it will beat around 2.5 billion times!

33: Muscles Can Adapt to Endurance or Strength

Different types of training develop different muscle qualities. Endurance training, like long-distance running, builds slow-twitch muscle fibers that can work for extended periods. Strength training, like weightlifting, builds fast-twitch fibers designed for short, powerful bursts of energy.

34: Your Eye Muscles Are the Busiest

The muscles controlling your eyes are the most active in the body. They move over 100,000 times a day as they help you focus and track objects.

35: Muscles Use Energy Even When You're at Rest

Your muscles continue to burn calories even when you're not actively using them. This is one reason why having more muscle mass can boost your metabolism.

36: The Smallest Muscle in the Body Is in the Ear

The stapedius, the smallest muscle in the human body, is located in your middle ear. It helps control the vibration of the stapes bone to protect the ear from loud noises.

37: Muscle Memory Is Real

Muscle memory is a phenomenon where your muscles "remember" certain movements after you've practiced them repeatedly. That's why skills like riding a bike or playing an instrument stay with you, even after a long time without practice.

38: Muscles Need Protein to Repair and Grow

Your muscles need protein to repair and rebuild After exercise. This is why athletes and fitness enthusiasts often consume protein-rich foods or supplements after a workout.

39: Your Body Loses Muscle Mass with Age

Starting in your 30s, your body gradually loses muscle mass in a process called sarcopenia. Regular strength training and physical activity can help slow this process and maintain muscle strength.

40: Muscle Endurance and Strength Aren't the Same

Strength refers to how much force a muscle can exert in one go, while endurance refers to how long a muscle can sustain repeated contractions over time. Different types of training target each quality.

41: Muscles Are More Powerful Than You Think

Under extreme stress, such as during emergencies, muscles can exert more force than normal, a phenomenon known as "hysterical strength." This has been seen in stories where people have lifted heavy objects to rescue others in danger.

42: You Can't "Bulk Up" from Cardio Alone

While cardio exercises like running or swimming are great for heart health and endurance, they won't significantly increase muscle size. Strength training, on the other hand, targets muscle growth and bulk.

43: Muscle Soreness Isn't Always a Sign of a Good Workout

While many people think muscle soreness after a workout means progress, it's not the only indicator. Soreness can occur from new or intense movements but isn't necessary for muscle growth.

44: Muscles Need Oxygen to Perform

During exercise, your muscles rely on oxygen to produce the energy they need to keep contracting. This is why your heart rate and breathing increase during physical activity to supply more oxygen to your working muscles.

45: The Longest Muscle Is the Sartorius

The sartorius muscle runs from the hip down to the inner part of the knee. It's the longest muscle in the body and helps you rotate your leg into a cross-legged position.

46: Muscles Can Tire in Seconds or Last Hours

Depending on the type of activity, muscles can tire out quickly or keep going for hours. Fast-twitch muscles, responsible for explosive power, tire out faster, while slow-twitch muscles can sustain long-duration activities like distance running.

47: Muscles Act in Pairs

Muscles usually work in pairs called agonists and antagonists. When one muscle contracts, the other relaxes.

48: Muscles Make Up About 40% of Body Weight

Muscles account for approximately 40% of your body weight. The exact percentage varies depending on factors like age, gender, and fitness level.

49: Muscles Can Grow Without Increasing Strength

It's possible for muscles to increase in size (hypertrophy) without a corresponding increase in strength, especially when using high-repetition training. This is because muscle size and strength are influenced by different factors.

50: Muscle Tone vs. Muscle Strength

Muscle tone is the progressive and non resistant partial compression of the muscles, which helps maintain a good posture.

Muscle strength, on the other hand, is the maximum amount of force a muscle can exert.

51: Muscles Can Work Without Oxygen

During high-intensity exercise, muscles can produce energy without oxygen through a process called anaerobic metabolism. This process produces lactic acid, which can lead to muscle fatigue.

52: Muscle Fibers Can Change Type

With training, muscle fibers can shift from one type to another. For example, endurance training can increase the proportion of slow-twitch fibers, while strength training can increase fast-twitch fibers.

53: Muscle Cramps Are Common and Varied

Muscle cramps are sudden, involuntary contractions that can occur during exercise or rest. They can be caused by dehydration, overuse, or imbalances in electrolytes like potassium and sodium.

54: Stretching Improves Muscle Flexibility

Regular stretching improves muscle flexibility, which can enhance performance and reduce the risk of injuries. Flexibility allows muscles and tendons to lengthen and handle stress more effectively.

55: Muscles Can Store Energy

Muscles store energy in the form of glycogen, which is a readily available source of energy during physical activity. Muscles can store about 400 grams of glycogen, primarily in the liver and muscle tissue.

56: Muscle Strength Declines with Age

As people age, muscle strength and mass naturally decline—a process known as sarcopenia. Regular exercise, especially strength training, can help mitigate this decline and maintain muscle function.

57: Muscle Growth Requires Rest

Muscles need time to recover and grow stronger after exercise. This is why rest days are crucial in any workout regimen, as they allow muscles to repair and rebuild.

58: The Brain Plays a Role in Muscle Control

Your brain controls muscle contractions through electrical signals sent via the nervous system. This coordination is essential for precise movements and overall motor control.

59: Muscle Endurance Is Key for Long-Distance Activities

Muscle endurance is the ability of muscles to perform sustained exercise over time. It is crucial for activities like marathon running or long-distance cycling, where muscles must work efficiently for extended periods.

60: Your Tongue Is a Muscle

The tongue is a muscle with impressive strength and dexterity. It helps with speaking, eating, and swallowing, and is covered in taste buds that contribute to your sense of taste.

61: Muscles Can "Remember" Previous Workouts

Muscle memory refers to the phenomenon where previously trained muscles can regain their size and strength more quickly than if starting from scratch. This is due to changes at the cellular level that persist even after periods of inactivity.

62: Muscles Need Hydration to Function Properly

Adequate hydration is crucial for muscle function. Water helps maintain muscle elasticity, prevents cramping, and supports the delivery of nutrients to muscle cells.

63: Muscles Can Generate Heat

Muscles generate heat as a byproduct of energy production. This heat helps maintain body temperature, especially during physical activity, and is why you feel warmer when you exercise.

64: Different Muscles Have Different Functions

Muscles are specialized for various functions. For instance, the biceps are designed for lifting and pulling actions, while the quadriceps are crucial for extending the knee and propelling movement.

65: The Strength of Muscles Can Be Measured

Muscle strength is often measured using tools like dynamometers or through exercises like the bench press or squat. These measurements help assess muscular health and track progress.

66: Muscles Play a Role in Breathing

Muscles such as the diaphragm and intercostals (between the ribs) are essential for breathing. They contract and relax to expand and contract the lungs, allowing air to flow in and out.

67: Muscles Adapt Quickly to Training

Muscles are highly adaptable to exercise. With consistent training, they can quickly increase in

strength and endurance, responding to the
demands placed upon them

SKIN FACTS

The Largest Organ and Its Wonders
Your skin is much more than just a protective covering; it's a dynamic and versatile organ that plays a vital role in regulating body temperature, sensation, and much more. As the largest organ in your body, your skin has incredible abilities to heal, protect, and adapt to the environment. Let's explore the wonders of this fascinating organ.

68: The Skin Is the Body's Largest Organ

The skin is the body's largest organ, covering an average area of about 22 square feet. It accounts for roughly 15% of your total body weight.

69: Three Layers of Protection

Your skin is made up of three main layers: the epidermis(external subcaste), dermis(middle subcaste), and hypodermis(deepest subcaste).
. Each layer has specific functions, from protection to storing fat.

70: Skin Sheds Thousands of Cells Daily

Every minute, you lose between 30,000 to 40,000 dead skin cells. Over the course of a year, this amounts to nearly 9 pounds of skin that your body sheds naturally!

71: It Takes About a Month for Skin to Renew

Your skin cells are constantly regenerating. It takes about 28 days for new skin cells to travel from the lowest layer of the epidermis to the surface, where they die and are eventually shed.

72: Your Skin Has Around 2 Million Sweat Glands

The average person has between 2 to 4 million sweat glands, with the highest concentration in the palms of the hands, soles of the feet, and armpits. These glands help regulate body temperature by releasing sweat when you're hot.

73: Skin Color Is Determined by Melanin

The pigment melanin is responsible for the color of your skin.

People with darker skin have further melanin, while those with lighter skin have lower. Melanin also helps cover your skin from dangerous UV rays.

74: Your Skin Is Waterproof

One of the skin's most amazing features is that it's waterproof! The top layer of your skin, called the stratum corneum, is made up of dead cells and a mixture of oils that form a barrier to keep water out and retain moisture.

75: The Skin Is a Sensory Organ

Your skin contains millions of nerve endings that help you sense touch, pressure, pain, and temperature. These sensations allow you to interact with your environment and protect you from potential harm.

76: Skin Can Heal Itself

When you cut or scrape your skin, it immediately begins to repair itself. Special cells called fibroblasts produce collagen, which acts as a scaffold for new tissue growth.

77: The Thinnest and Thickest Skin

The skin on your eyelids is the thinnest at just 0.5 mm, while the thickest skin is on the soles of your feet and the palms of your hands, measuring up to 4 mm thick.

78: Your Skin Is a Shield Against Germs

Your skin acts as a physical barrier against harmful pathogens like bacteria, viruses, and fungi. It's your body's first line of defense in keeping out unwanted invaders.

79: UV Rays Can Damage Skin Even on Cloudy Days

Ultraviolet (UV) rays from the sun can penetrate through clouds, which means your skin can still be exposed to harmful radiation even when it's overcast. Wearing sunscreen year-round is important for skin health.

80: Your Skin's Acid Mantle

The surface of your skin has a thin, slightly acidic layer called the acid mantle, which helps prevent the growth of harmful bacteria and fungi. This protective barrier also helps maintain moisture.

81: The Skin Contains Natural Antibiotics

Your skin produces natural antimicrobial proteins that help fight infections. These proteins help keep the skin free from harmful microbes, making it an essential part of your immune system.

82: Goosebumps Are a Throwback to Our Ancestors

When you're cold or scared, tiny muscles in your skin cause your hair to stand up, creating goosebumps. This reaction was more useful for our ancestors, who had more body hair, as it helped trap heat and made them appear larger to predators.

83: Freckles and Moles Are Collections of Pigment

Freckles and moles are small, concentrated areas of melanin, the pigment that gives skin its color. Freckles tend to increase with sun exposure, while moles are usually present from birth or develop over time.

84: The Skin Can Show Signs of Internal Health Issues

Your skin can reflect your overall health. Conditions like dehydration, liver disease, and certain vitamin deficiencies can manifest as dryness, discoloration, or rashes on the skin.

85: Scar Tissue Is Different from Normal Skin

When your skin heals from an injury, the resulting scar tissue is made up of a different type of collagen than normal skin. This is why scars often look different in color and texture from the surrounding skin.

86: Skin Plays a Role in Vitamin D Production

When exposed to sunlight, your skin helps produce vitamin D, which is essential for strong bones and overall health. However, too much sun exposure without protection can lead to skin damage.

87: Aging and Your Skin

As you age, your skin naturally loses elasticity and moisture, leading to wrinkles and sagging. Protecting your skin from sun exposure, staying hydrated, and using moisturizers can help slow the aging process.

88: Skin Has Its Own Immune System

The skin has its own immune defense system, including specialized cells like Langerhans cells that help detect and fight off pathogens, contributing to the body's overall immune response.

89: Skin Can Absorb Substances

The skin is capable of absorbing various substances, including medications in the form of topical treatments. This property is why certain drugs are applied directly to the skin for localized effects.

90: Skin Color Can Change with Temperature

Skin color can temporarily change based on temperature. For example, when you're cold, your skin may appear pale due to constricted blood vessels, while blushing or overheating can make your skin look redder.

91: Your Skin Is Home to Millions of Microorganisms

The skin hosts a diverse community of microorganisms, including bacteria, fungi, and viruses. These microbes form the skin microbiome, which plays a role in protecting against harmful pathogens and maintaining skin health.

92: The Skin's Ability to Heal Varies by Age

The skin's ability to heal from wounds and injuries can vary with age. Younger skin tends to heal faster due to higher collagen production, while older skin may take longer to repair due to decreased collagen and elastin.

93: Your Skin Can Detect Changes in Environmental Conditions

The skin is equipped with receptors that can sense changes in environmental conditions, such as temperature, humidity, and pressure. These receptors help the body adapt to different environments and protect itself.

94: Skin Can Reflect Emotional States

Your skin can reflect emotional states and stress levels. For example, stress or anxiety can trigger skin conditions like acne or eczema, while feelings of happiness can lead to a healthy, glowing complexion.

95: Skin Sensitivity Varies by Area

For instance, the skin on your fingertips is highly sensitive to touch due to a high concentration of nerve endings, while the skin on your back is less sensitive.

96: Sun Exposure Affects Skin Aging

Prolonged exposure to ultraviolet (UV) radiation from the sun can accelerate skin aging, leading to wrinkles, age spots, and loss of elasticity. Wearing sunscreen and protective clothing can help mitigate these effects.

97: The Skin Has Its Own Natural Moisturizers

Your skin produces natural moisturizers, including sebum (an oily substance) and ceramides (fatty molecules). These help keep the skin hydrated and maintain its barrier function.

98: Skin Can Produce Vitamin D Efficiently

Exposure to sunlight allows the skin to produce vitamin D, which is essential for bone health and immune function. The skin converts UVB rays into vitamin D, making it an important part of maintaining overall health.

99: Skin Sensitivity Can Change with Hormones

Hormonal changes, such as those occurring during puberty, pregnancy, or menopause, can affect skin sensitivity and condition. For example, hormonal fluctuations can lead to acne or changes in skin texture.

100: Skin Thickness Varies Across the Body

Skin thickness varies significantly across the body. The thinnest skin is on the eyelids, while the thickest skin is on the soles of the feet and palms of the hands, providing extra protection in high-wear areas.

101: Skin Can Develop Tolerance to Certain Products

Over time, skin can develop tolerance to certain skincare products, which might reduce their effectiveness. It's often recommended to periodically adjust skincare routines to maintain optimal results.

102: The Skin's Color Can Reflect Health Conditions

For example, yellowing of the skin may suggest liver issues, while a bluish tint might indicate poor oxygenation or circulation problems.

103: Your Skin Produces More Oil in Humid Conditions

In high humidity, your skin may produce more oil, which can lead to a greasy appearance and potentially exacerbate conditions like acne. Maintaining a balanced skincare routine can help manage oil production.

104: The Skin's Elasticity Decreases with Age

As you age, the skin's elasticity decreases due to a reduction in collagen and elastin fibers. This loss of elasticity contributes to the formation of wrinkles and sagging skin.

105: Skin Can Store Melanin for Sun Protection

When exposed to sunlight, the skin produces more melanin to protect itself from UV damage. This increased melanin gives the skin a tan, which acts as a natural form of sun protection.

106: The Skin Is Involved in Temperature Regulation

When you're hot, sweat evaporates from the skin to cool the body, and blood vessels expand to release excess heat.

107: Skin Can Experience a "Glow" from Hydration

Well-hydrated skin often has a healthy, radiant glow. Drinking plenty of water and using moisturizing products can improve skin hydration and appearance.

EYES FACTS

108: You Have a Blind Spot

The human eye has a small blind spot where the optic nerve connects to the retina. This spot lacks photoreceptors, but your brain fills in the gap, making you unaware of it in everyday life.

109: The Eye Can Distinguish Over 10 Million Colors

Human eyes are capable of detecting approximately 10 million different colors, thanks to the three types of color-detecting cells in the retina called cones.

110: Your Eyes Blink About 15-20 Times Per Minute

On average, you blink about 15-20 times per minute to keep your eyes moist and protected from irritants. This blinking helps to spread tears evenly across the eye surface.

111: The Human Eye Can Focus on 50 Different Things Per Second

Your eyes can shift focus rapidly between different objects, allowing you to process up to 50 different images per second. This rapid focusing helps you track moving objects and read quickly.

112: Eyes Have the Fastest Muscles in the Body

The muscles controlling your eye movements are the fastest muscles in the body. They can move your eyes at speeds of up to 900 degrees per second.

113: Your Eyes Are About the Size of a Ping-Pong Ball

The average adult eye is roughly 1 inch (2.5 cm) in diameter, about the size of a ping-pong ball. Despite their small size, they have an incredibly complex structure.

114: Each Eye Has Around 120 Million Rods and 6 Million Cones

The retina in each eye contains around 120 million rod cells, which are sensitive to low light and help with night vision, and about 6 million cone cells, which detect color and fine detail.

115: Your Eyes Can Adjust to Different Light Levels in Seconds

Your eyes have the remarkable ability to adjust to varying light levels. In bright light, your pupils constrict to protect the retina, while in low light, they dilate to allow more light in.

116: Eyes Can Change Color

While the color of your eyes is mostly determined by genetics, it can change slightly due to factors like age, lighting, or certain health conditions.

117: Eye Color Is Unique to Each Individual

Just like fingerprints, the combination of eye color, texture, and patterns is unique to each person. Even identical twins can have different eye patterns.

118: Your Eyes Can Detect Light from a Single Candle

Under ideal dark conditions, your eyes are sensitive enough to detect the light from a single candle burning 30 miles away. This remarkable sensitivity allows you to see in very low light conditions.

119: The Cornea Is the Only Tissue in the Body That Has No Blood Supply

The cornea, the clear front part of the eye, is unique in that it does not have a blood supply. Instead, it receives nutrients directly from tears and the aqueous humor, which helps keep it transparent.

120: Your Eyes Have Built-In Sun Protection

Your eyes have natural mechanisms to protect themselves from excessive sunlight. The iris adjusts the size of the pupil to limit light entry, and the eye produces tears to wash out harmful particles.

121: The Human Eye Can Process 36,000 Bits of Information Per Hour

Your eyes can process an impressive amount of visual information. They send around 36,000 bits of data to the brain each hour, allowing you to perceive and interpret your surroundings in detail.

122: Your Eyes Are Almost the Same Size at Birth and in Adulthood

The size of your eyes remains relatively constant from birth through adulthood. While the rest of your body grows significantly, your eyes' size increases only slightly during childhood.

123: The Eye's Retina Contains About 6 Million Cone Cells

color vision and detailed central vision are the responsibility of the Cone cells in the retina. retina's 6 million cone cells enable you to perceive a wide range of colors and fine details.

124: Each Eye Has a Different Color Spectrum

Each eye can perceive slightly different color spectra due to variations in individual cone cells. This means that each person's perception of color can be unique to their own visual system.

125: Your Eyes Can Adjust to Seeing Underwater

While humans can't see clearly underwater due to the refractive index of water, your eyes can adapt somewhat by adjusting the lens curvature. However, without special lenses or goggles, vision remains blurry.

126: Eye Color Can Change with Mood

While not a permanent change, eye color can appear to shift based on emotions or lighting. Pupils dilate in low light or excitement, making the iris appear darker or lighter depending on the surrounding light.

127: Humans Have Three Types of Cones for Color Vision

There are three types of cone cells in the retina, each sensitive to different wavelengths of light (red, green, and blue). The combination of these cones allows for the perception of a full spectrum of colors.

128: Your Eyes Can Detect Rapid Movements

The human eye is capable of detecting rapid movements and changes in the environment. This ability is crucial for activities such as driving or playing sports, where quick reflexes are necessary.

129: The Eye Can Adapt to Different Viewing Distances

The eye's lens can change its shape to focus on objects at varying distances, a process known as accommodation. This adaptability allows you to switch from viewing something close up to something far away seamlessly.

130: Your Peripheral Vision Is More Sensitive to Light

The peripheral vision (side vision) is more sensitive to light and motion than central vision. This sensitivity helps detect movement and potential threats from the side, which is essential for survival in the wild.

131: The Human Eye Is Capable of Night Vision

While not as advanced as nocturnal animals, human eyes have some night vision capabilities due to the presence of rod cells in the retina, which are highly sensitive to low light levels.

132: Your Eyes Can Improve Vision with Age

Contrary to common belief, some people experience improved distance vision as they age due to changes in the lens's elasticity. However, this often comes with a decline in near vision, known as presbyopia.

133: The Eyeball Is a Spherical Structure

The eyeball is roughly spherical in shape, with a diameter of about 1 inch (2.5 cm). This spherical shape is crucial for the eye's ability to focus light onto the retina properly.

134: Your Eyes Have a Natural "Filter"

The lens of the eye acts as a natural filter, blocking some of the UV rays from reaching the retina. This protection helps prevent UV-related damage and contributes to long-term eye health.

135: Eye Color Can Affect How Much Light Is Absorbed

Lighter-colored eyes, such as blue or green, tend to absorb less light compared to darker-colored eyes. This means that individuals with lighter eyes may experience more sensitivity to bright lights.

136: Eyes Can Function Independently

Each eye can function independently, allowing you to focus on different objects simultaneously. This independence helps with depth perception and peripheral vision.

137: Humans Have Better Color Vision Than Most Animals

While some animals have superior night vision or a broader visual range, humans typically have better color vision due to the presence of three types of cone cells that allow for a rich spectrum of colors.

EARS FACTS

138: The Ear Is Divided into Three Parts

The ear is divided into three main parts: the outer ear (auricle and ear canal), the middle ear (eardrum and ossicles), and the inner ear (cochlea and vestibular system). Each part plays a role in hearing and balance.

139: The Smallest Bone in the Body Is in the Ear

The smallest bone in the human body is the stapes, which is found in the middle ear. It measures just around 0.1 inches (2.5 mm) and plays a crucial role in transmitting sound vibrations to the inner ear.

140: You Can Hear Sounds as Low as 20 Hz and as High as 20,000 Hz

The human ear can detect sounds within a range of 20 Hz to 20,000 Hz. Sounds below 20 Hz are considered infrasound, and those above 20,000 Hz are ultrasound.

141: Your Ears Continue to Grow Throughout Your Life

Unlike most parts of your body, your ears continue to grow throughout your life due to the cartilage's natural tendency to elongate. This growth is usually subtle and occurs over many years.

142: The Ears Help Maintain Balance

The vestibular system, which is located in The inner ear, helps maintain balance and spatial orientation. It works with your eyes and brain to keep you upright and coordinated.

143: Earwax Has Protective Properties

The ears are protected by Earwax (cerumen) which protects the ear canal by trapping dust, debris, and microorganisms. The ears are also prevented from infection because of its antimicrobial properties.

144: Each Ear Can Hear Sounds Separately

Your brain processes sounds from each ear independently, which helps with sound localization. This ability allows you to determine the direction and distance of sounds more accurately.

145: You Can Have Different Hearing Sensitivities in Each Ear

It's common for people to have different hearing sensitivities in each ear, which can be influenced by factors such as age, noise exposure, or ear infections.

146: Your Ears Are Self-Cleaning

The ear canal has a natural self-cleaning mechanism. As earwax gradually moves out of the ear canal, it carries away dead skin cells and other debris, keeping the ear clean.

147: Hearing Loss Can Affect Balance

Hearing loss, particularly if it affects the inner ear, can impact balance and coordination. This is because the vestibular system in the inner ear is responsible for both hearing and balance.

148: The Ear Can Distinguish Between Over 1,000 Different Tones

The human ear is capable of distinguishing between over 1,000 different tones, allowing for the recognition of subtle differences in pitch and tone, which is essential for understanding speech and enjoying music.

149: Your Ears Can Adjust to Different Sound Intensities

The ear has a built-in mechanism to protect against loud noises called the acoustic reflex. Tiny muscles in the middle ear contract in response to loud sounds, reducing the amount of sound energy transmitted to the inner ear.

150: You Have Two Ears to Help with Sound Localization

Having two ears helps you localize sounds in your environment. By comparing the timing and volume of sounds reaching each ear, your brain can determine the direction and distance of the sound source.

151; The Eardrum Vibrates at the Same Frequency as the Sound

The eardrum vibrates in response to sound waves, and these vibrations are at the same frequency as the sound. This process allows sound waves to be converted into electrical signals that the brain can interpret.

152: Earwax Is Actually a Natural Antiseptic

Earwax (cerumen) contains antimicrobial properties that help to prevent infections in the ear canal. It also has a slightly acidic pH that inhibits the growth of bacteria and fungi.

153: Your Ears Can Continue to Hear While You Sleep

Even while you sleep, your ears continue to detect sounds. This ability allows you to wake up in response to important or dangerous sounds, such as an alarm or a baby crying.

154: The Inner Ear Is Also Responsible for Balance

The inner ear contains the vestibular system, which is responsible for maintaining balance and spatial orientation. It helps you stay upright and coordinate movements, working alongside visual and proprioceptive inputs.

155: The Ear Can Detect Sound Frequencies as Low as 20 Hz

The human ear can detect sound frequencies as low as 20 Hz, which corresponds to deep bass sounds. This sensitivity allows you to hear low-frequency noises, such as the rumble of thunder.

156: Your Ears Can Become "Clogged" by Pressure Changes

Changes in atmospheric pressure, such as during air travel or diving, can cause a sensation of pressure or fullness in the ears. This occurs because the Eustachian tube, which equalizes pressure, may become blocked.

157: The Shape of Your Ears Can Affect Hearing

The shape and size of the outer ear (auricle) can influence how sound waves are captured and directed into the ear canal. Variations in ear shape can slightly alter how sound is perceived.

158: Ears Have Their Own Natural Cleaning Mechanism

The ear canal has a natural self-cleaning process. Earwax is gradually pushed out of the ear canal by the movement of the jaw during activities like talking and chewing.

159: The Ear Can Experience "Sound Fatigue"

Prolonged exposure to loud sounds can lead to sound fatigue, where the ear becomes less sensitive to incoming sounds. This temporary condition usually recovers with rest and reduced exposure to loud noises.

160: Your Ear Can Detect Sound Direction Even with Your Eyes Closed

The brain uses the difference in the time it takes for sound to reach each ear and the intensity of the sound to determine its direction. This ability helps you locate sounds even when you cannot see them.

161: The Ear Is Involved in the Body's Equilibrium System

The equilibrium is maintained by The vestibular system in the inner ear. It helps coordinate movements and maintain posture by detecting changes in head position and motion.

162: The Ear's Cochlea Is Shaped Like a Spiral

The cochlea, a key structure in the inner ear responsible for converting sound vibrations into electrical signals, is shaped like a spiral. This spiral structure helps to separate different frequencies of sound.

163: The Outer Ear Can Amplify Sound by Up to 10 dB

The shape of the outer ear (auricle) helps capture and amplify sound waves before they enter the ear canal. This amplification can enhance the sensitivity of hearing by up to 10 decibels.

164: Hearing Loss Can Be Caused by Both Genetics and Environmental Factors

Hearing loss can result from genetic factors, such as congenital conditions, as well as environmental factors like prolonged exposure to loud noises or infections.

165: Your Ears Can Develop Tinnitus

The ringing or buzzing sounds in the ears without an external sound source is called tinnitus. It can be caused by factors such as hearing loss, ear infections, or exposure to loud noises.

166: The Eustachian Tube Helps Equalize Ear Pressure

The Eustachian tube connects the middle ear to the back of the throat and helps equalize pressure between the middle ear and the external environment. It opens when you swallow, yawn, or chew.

167: Ears Have Different Sensitivities at Different Frequencies

The sensitivity of the ear varies with frequency. Generally, the ear is most sensitive to frequencies in the mid-range, such as human speech, and less sensitive to very low or very high frequencies.

NOSE FACTS

168: The Nose Can Detect Over 1 Trillion Different Scents

The human nose is capable of detecting an astonishing range of smells. Recent research suggests that our olfactory system can distinguish over 1 trillion different odor molecules.

169: Your Sense of Smell Is Linked to Memory

The sense of smell is closely connected to the brain's limbic system, which is involved in emotion and memory. This is why certain smells can evoke vivid memories and strong emotions.

170: The Nose Has Its Own Unique Fingerprint

Just like fingerprints, each person's nose has a unique shape and structure. No two noses are exactly alike, which is why facial recognition systems often use nose shape as one of the identifying features.

171: You Can Smell Without Knowing It

Sometimes, people can detect smells without being consciously aware of them. This is known as subliminal odor perception and can influence moods and decisions without you realizing it.

172: The Nose Helps in Filtering and Humidifying Air

One of the primary functions of the nose is to filter, warm, and humidify the air you breathe. Tiny hairs and mucus in the nasal passages trap dust, germs, and other particles, protecting your lungs and respiratory system.

173: Your Nose Continues to Grow Throughout Your Life

Unlike other parts of the body, the nose continues to grow slowly throughout a person's life due to the cartilage's gradual elongation. This is why older adults often have larger noses compared to their younger selves.

174: The Nose Plays a Role in Enhancing Taste

Your sense of smell is closely connected to Your sense of taste. When you eat, aroma molecules travel to the olfactory receptors through the back of the throat, contributing to the overall flavor experience.

175: The Nose Can Help Detect Disease

Research has shown that certain diseases, like diabetes and Parkinson's disease, can cause distinctive changes in body odor. This ability of the nose to detect such changes can sometimes aid in early diagnosis.

176: Humans Have an Olfactory Memory

The human nose can remember smells with remarkable accuracy. Studies have shown that people can recognize and recall specific scents even years after first encountering them.

177: The Nose Has Olfactory Receptors for Different Odors

The human nose contains about 400 different types of olfactory receptors, each specialized to detect specific odor molecules. These receptors work together to create the perception of complex smells.

178: Your Nose Can Adapt to Constant Scents

The olfactory system can become accustomed to constant or repetitive odors over time. This phenomenon, known as olfactory adaptation, allows you to detect new or unusual smells more easily.

179: The Nose Is Involved in Regulating Breathing

The nasal passages play a role in regulating airflow and breathing patterns. Breathing through the nose helps to slow the breath rate and increase oxygen absorption compared to breathing through the mouth.

180: Nasal Congestion Affects Your Sense of Taste

When you have a cold or nasal congestion, your sense of taste is often diminished. This is because the blocked nasal passages limit the ability of aroma molecules to reach the olfactory receptors.

181: The Nose Has a Built-In Humidifier

The nasal mucosa contains glands that secrete mucus to keep the airways moist. This mucus helps to prevent dryness in the respiratory system and protects the lungs from irritation.

182: Your Nose Can Influence Your Voice

The shape and structure of your nasal passages contribute to the quality and resonance of your voice. Changes in nasal passages, such as those caused by congestion or surgery, can alter how your voice sounds.

183: The Nose Can Detect Danger

The sense of smell is linked to instinctive responses. For example, the detection of a foul odor or smoke can trigger immediate alertness and protective behaviors.

184: The Nose Is Sensitive to Temperature Changes

The nasal passages are sensitive to temperature changes, which can affect the perception of smells. Cold air can reduce the sense of smell, while warm air can enhance it.

185: The Nose Can Influence Your Emotions

Smell can have a powerful impact on emotions. Certain scents, like lavender or vanilla, are known to have calming effects, while others, like peppermint or citrus, can be invigorating.

186: The Nose and Sinuses Are Linked

The nasal passages are connected to the sinuses, which are air-filled cavities in the skull. The health of the sinuses can affect nasal congestion and the overall function of the nose.

187: The Nose Has a Built-In Defense Mechanism

The nose has several defense mechanisms, including sneezing and coughing, to expel irritants and pathogens. This reflex helps to protect the lungs from dangerous substances.

188: The Nose Is a Key Player in Immune Defense

The nose helps to protect the body from pathogens by trapping and filtering out bacteria, viruses, and other microorganisms through mucus and the nasal hairs.

189: Each Nostril Has Its Own Sense of Smell

Research has shown that each nostril can have slightly different olfactory sensitivity. This means you might detect different smells more strongly in one nostril compared to the other.

190: The Sense of Smell Can Influence Appetite

The aroma of food can significantly affect appetite and food choices. Pleasant smells can increase appetite and make food more appealing, while unpleasant smells can reduce hunger.

191: The Nose Plays a Role in Air Conditioning

The nose acts as a natural air conditioner by warming and humidifying the air before it reaches the lungs. This helps to prevent respiratory irritation and maintains optimal lung function.

192: Smelling is an Instant Reaction

Unlike other senses, the sense of smell is processed very quickly by the brain. This rapid processing allows you to detect and react to potentially harmful or beneficial odors almost instantaneously.

193: Humans Have a Limited Sense of Smell Compared to Animals

While humans have a highly developed sense of smell, it is not as acute as that of some animals. For example, dogs have significantly more olfactory receptors, making their sense of smell far more sensitive.

194: Nasal Septum Separates the Nostrils

The cartilage and bone structure that divides the nasal cavity into two nostrils is The nasal septum .

A deviated septum can affect airflow and contribute to breathing difficulties.

195: The Nose Can Be Affected by Allergies

Allergic reactions can cause inflammation and increased mucus production in the nasal passages. Common allergens include pollen, dust, and pet dander, leading to symptoms like sneezing and congestion.

196: The Nose Is Sensitive to Chemical Irritants

The olfactory system can detect and react to chemical irritants such as smoke, strong perfumes, and cleaning agents. Exposure to these substances can cause discomfort and potentially harm the nasal lining.

197: Smell Can Influence Emotional Well-being

Pleasant scents, like lavender or rosemary, are often used in aromatherapy to promote relaxation and reduce stress. Conversely, unpleasant odors can trigger negative emotional responses and discomfort.

198: The Nose Plays a Role in Speech Production

The nasal cavity contributes to the resonance and quality of your voice. Changes in the nasal passages, such as those caused by a cold or sinus infection, can affect how your voice sounds.

199: The Sense of Smell Deteriorates with Age

As people age, their sense of smell can diminish due to a decrease in the number of olfactory receptors and changes in the olfactory bulb. This decline can impact taste and overall enjoyment of food.

200: The Nose Can Be Trained to Detect Specific Scents

The sense of smell can be trained and improved through practice. For example, perfumers and sommeliers often undergo training to refine their ability to detect and identify specific scents and flavors.

201: Nasal Breathing Affects Overall Health

Breathing through the nose rather than the mouth is generally healthier. Nasal breathing helps to filter and warm the air, regulate airflow, and engage the diaphragm more effectively.

202: The Nose Has a Role in Sleep Quality

Nasal congestion or other breathing issues can impact sleep quality. Conditions such as sleep apnea can be influenced by nasal health, affecting overall rest and well-being.

203: The Nose Can Influence Mood and Behavior

Certain scents can influence mood and behavior. For example, the smell of fresh-cut grass can evoke feelings of happiness and nostalgia, while unpleasant odors can create a sense of unease.

204: The Nose Contains Specialized Receptors for Odors

The nasal cavity contains specialized olfactory receptors that are sensitive to different types of odor molecules. These receptors are responsible for detecting and distinguishing between various smells.

205: The Nose Can React to Environmental Changes

Changes in environmental conditions, such as temperature and humidity, can affect the sensitivity and function of the nose. For example, dry air can lead to nasal dryness and irritation.

206: The Nose Plays a Role in Filtering Out Pollution

The nose helps to filter out particulate matter and pollutants from the air before it reaches the lungs. This function is crucial for reducing the impact of environmental pollutants on respiratory health.

207: The Sense of Smell Can Be Affected by Certain Medications

Some medications can alter or diminish the sense of smell as a side effect. For example, certain antibiotics and antihistamines can impact olfactory function and perception.

FACTS ON HAIR AND NAILS

208: Hair Growth Rate

On average, human hair grows about half an inch (1.25 cm) per month. This equates to roughly 6 inches (15 cm) per year, although growth rates can vary depending on factors like genetics and health.

209: Hair Follicles Are Everywhere

Hair follicles are distributed across most of the body, except for the palms of your hands, soles of your feet, and lips. The density of hair follicles can vary, with some areas having more follicles than others.

210: Hair is Primarily Made of Keratin

Hair is composed mainly of a protein called keratin. This durable protein helps protect hair from damage and contributes to its strength and structure.

211: The Average Number of Hair Strands

The average human head has about 100,000 to 150,000 hair strands. People with blonde hair typically have more strands compared to those with darker hair.

212: Hair Color Comes from Melanin

Hair color is determined by melanin, the same pigment that affects skin color. The amount and type of melanin (eumelanin or pheomelanin) in the hair follicle determine whether hair is black, brown, blonde, or red.

213 Hair Can Grow in Cycles

Three phases make up a hair development cycle: telogen (resting), catagen (transition), and anagen (growing). Every hair strand experiences these stages on its own.

214: The Oldest Known Hair Sample

The oldest known human hair sample dates back to approximately 9,000 years ago. This ancient hair was preserved in permafrost and provides valuable insights into early human life.

215: Scalp Hair Loss

On average, people lose about 50 to 100 hair strands per day. This natural process of shedding is typically balanced by new hair growth.

216: The Role of Hair in Temperature Regulation

Hair helps to regulate body temperature by providing insulation. It acts as a barrier to prevent heat loss from the body, especially in cold weather.

217: Hair Growth Can Be Affected by Diet

A balanced diet rich in vitamins and minerals, such as iron, biotin, and zinc, can support healthy hair growth. Deficiencies in these nutrients can lead to hair thinning or loss.

218: Hair Is the Fastest-Growing Tissue in the Human Body

Hair is the fastest-growing tissue in the human body, second only to bone marrow, expanding 6 inches (15 cm) on average every year.

219: The Average Lifespan of a Hair Strand

 A hair strand can live for two to seven years. The length of the hair growth cycle varies from person to person and is influenced by genetics, health, and age.

220: Hair Density Can Vary by Color

People with blonde hair generally have the highest density of hair follicles, with an average of around 150,000 follicles. Brunettes typically have around 100,000, while those with red hair have fewer, approximately 90,000 follicles.

221: Hair and Health Connection

Changes in hair health can sometimes signal underlying health issues. For example, sudden hair loss or changes in hair texture can be a sign of nutritional deficiencies, hormonal imbalances, or other health conditions.

222: Human Hair Is Stronger Than Steel

A single strand of human hair can support up to 100 grams (3.5 ounces) of weight. This makes it significantly stronger than a comparable thickness of steel.

223: Hair Can Be Used for Forensic Analysis

Hair can provide valuable forensic information. The analysis of hair samples can help identify individuals, determine drug use, or even reveal exposure to environmental toxins.

224: Hair Growth Is Affected by Seasons

Hair growth rates can fluctuate with the seasons. Studies have shown that hair tends to grow faster in the summer and slower in the winter due to factors like increased sunlight and overall metabolic activity.

225: Hair Has Different Textures

Hair texture can vary widely from person to person and includes straight, wavy, curly, and coiled types. The shape of the hair follicle determines the texture, with round follicles producing straight hair and oval-shaped follicles producing curly hair.

226: Stress Can Affect Hair Growth

High levels of stress can lead to a condition known as telogen effluvium, where a large number of hair follicles enter the resting phase simultaneously, causing temporary hair loss.

227: Hair Color Can Change with Age

As people age, their hair often changes color due to the gradual reduction in melanin production. This can lead to graying or whitening of the hair over time.

228: Hair Can Absorb and Retain Chemicals

Hair has the ability to absorb and retain various chemicals, including pollutants and drugs. This characteristic makes it a useful tool for detecting substance abuse or environmental exposure.

229: Hair Growth Rate Varies Across the Body

Different parts of the body have varying hair growth rates. For example, scalp hair grows faster than body hair, and facial hair typically grows at a different rate than scalp hair.

230: Hair Health Can Be Affected by Diet

A diet rich in vitamins and minerals, such as vitamins A, C, D, E, biotin, and omega-3 fatty acids, supports healthy hair growth and helps maintain its strength and elasticity.

231: Hair Loss is Normal

It is normal to lose between 50 to 100 hair strands daily as part of the natural hair renewal process. Excessive hair loss beyond this range can indicate potential issues.

232: Hair Can Be Affected by Hormones

Changes in hormones can significantly impact hair growth and health. Conditions such as pregnancy, menopause, and thyroid disorders can lead to changes in hair texture, density, and growth patterns.

233: Hair Follicles Can Be Repaired

Damage to hair follicles can sometimes be repaired through treatments such as medications, topical applications, and lifestyle changes. Early intervention is key to promoting healthy hair growth.

234: Hair Can Act as a Barometer for Health

Hair can provide insights into overall health and wellness. For example, changes in hair texture or color can be indicators of nutritional deficiencies, hormonal imbalances, or other systemic health issues.

235: Hair Loss Patterns Differ by Gender

Hair loss patterns can differ between genders. Men often experience a receding hairline and bald spots, while women usually experience diffuse thinning across the scalp.

236: Hair Can Be Used in Drug Testing

Hair samples can be used for drug testing because drugs and their metabolites can remain in hair for months after use, providing a longer window of detection compared to blood or urine tests.

237: Hair is an Important Cultural Symbol

Throughout history, hair has held cultural and symbolic significance in many societies. Hair styles and grooming practices can signify social status, religious beliefs, and personal identity.

NAIL FACTS

238: Nails Are Made of Keratin

Like hair, nails are primarily composed of keratin. This protein gives nails their strength and resilience, helping them protect the fingertips and toes.

239: Nails Grow Faster in Warmer Months

Fingernails tend to grow faster in warmer months and slower in colder months. This seasonal variation is influenced by factors such as blood flow and metabolic rate.

240: Nail Growth Rate

Fingernails grow about 1/8 inch (3 mm) per month, while toenails grow more slowly, about 1/16 inch (1.5 mm) per month. The growth rate can be influenced by age, health, and nutrition.

241: Nails Can Reflect Health Issues

Health issues can be indicated through Changes in nail color, shape, or texture. For example, yellowing nails might suggest fungal infections, while pale nails can be a sign of anemia.

242: The Hardest Part of the Nail

The part of the nail that is most visible and hardened is called the nail plate. It is made up of layers of keratinized cells and protects the softer tissues underneath.

243: Nail Beds Are Sensitive

The area under the nail, known as the nail bed, is rich in blood vessels and nerve endings, making it sensitive to touch and pressure.

244: Nails Grow Continuously

Unlike hair, nails grow continuously and do not stop growing unless damaged or if growth is interrupted by illness or injury.

245: The Average Number of Nails

Most people have 20 nails in total: 10 fingernails and 10 toenails. However, some individuals may have extra or fewer nails due to genetic conditions or abnormalities.

246: The Nail Matrix

The nail matrix is the tissue located under the base of the nail (cuticle) that produces new cells, which become the nail plate. It plays a crucial role in nail growth.

247: Nail Care and Hygiene

Proper nail care and hygiene are important for preventing infections and maintaining nail health. Regular trimming, moisturizing, and avoiding harsh chemicals can help keep nails in good condition.

248: Nails Grow Faster in Children and Young Adults

Nails typically grow faster in children and young adults compared to older adults. As people age, their nail growth rate can slow down due to changes in metabolism and overall health.

249: The Lunula is the White Crescent Shape

The white, crescent-shaped area at the base of the nail is the lunula. It is the visible part of the nail matrix and is often more prominent on the thumb than on other fingers.

250: Nail Color Can Indicate Health Issues

Nails can reflect various health conditions:

Blue Nails: May indicate a lack of oxygen or circulatory problems.
Purple Nails: Could signal poor circulation or a heart condition.
White Nails: Sometimes associated with liver conditions like hepatitis.
Red Nails: May suggest inflammation or infection.
Nails and Fingernails Can Be Used for Identification
Just like fingerprints, nails can be unique to individuals. Forensic experts sometimes use nail patterns and characteristics for identification purposes in criminal investigations.

251: Nail Biting Can Affect Nail Health

Habitual nail biting can lead to various problems, including infections, nail deformities, and damage to the surrounding skin. It can also cause the nail to grow irregularly.

252: Toenails Grow More Slowly Than Fingernails

Toenails grow at a slower rate than fingernails. On average, toenails take about 12 to 18 months to completely regrow, compared to 6 to 8 months for fingernails.

253: Nail Fungus is Common

Fungal infections of the nails (onychomycosis) are common and can cause discoloration, thickening, and brittleness. They are more likely to occur in warm, moist environments and among individuals with weakened immune systems.

254: Nail Polish and Health

Regular use of nail polish can sometimes lead to problems if the polish is not properly removed or if the nails are not given time to breathe. Some nail polishes contain chemicals that may cause allergic reactions or nail damage.

255: The Hardest Part of the Nail is the Nail Plate

The nail plate, the hard, visible part of the nail, is composed of layers of keratinized cells. Despite its hardness, it can be prone to damage from trauma or harsh chemicals.

256: Nails Can Grow Differently on Each Hand

Nail growth rates and patterns can vary between hands. Typically, nails on the dominant hand (the hand you use more frequently) may grow slightly faster due to increased blood flow and use.

257: Nail Growth Can Be Affected by Diet

Healthy nail growth is supported by A diet rich in proteins, vitamins, and minerals. Nutrients such as biotin, zinc, and omega-3 fatty acids are particularly important for maintaining strong and healthy nails.

258: Nail Plate Thickness Varies

The thickness of the nail plate can vary from person to person and between different nails on the same individual. Thicker nails may be more resilient but can also be more prone to fungal infections.

259: Nail Changes Can Indicate Nutritional Deficiencies

Changes in nail appearance, such as ridges or discoloration, can sometimes signal nutritional deficiencies. For example, horizontal ridges might indicate a zinc deficiency, while white spots could be related to a calcium deficiency.

260: Nail Growth Is Influenced by Age and Hormones

Hormonal changes, such as those occurring during pregnancy or menopause, can affect nail growth and appearance. Age also plays a role, with nails often becoming more brittle and slower to grow as people get older.

261: Nail Care is Essential for Overall Health

Proper nail care, including regular trimming, cleaning, and moisturizing, helps prevent issues like infections, ingrown nails, and splitting. It also contributes to overall hand hygiene and health.

262: Nail Salons Must Follow Strict Hygiene Practices

Professional nail salons are required to follow strict hygiene practices to prevent the spread of infections and diseases. This includes sanitizing tools, using disposable items when possible, and maintaining a clean environment.

263: Nail Growth Patterns Can Be Affected by Stress

Physical or emotional stress can impact nail growth and health. Stress may lead to conditions like nail thinning, vertical ridges, or even temporary nail loss.

264: Nails Can Show Signs of Dehydration

Dry, brittle nails can be a sign of dehydration or inadequate moisture levels. Regularly applying moisturizers and maintaining adequate hydration can help improve nail health.

265: Nails Are More Likely to Break in Winter

Cold, dry winter weather can lead to dry and brittle nails, making them more prone to breaking and splitting. Moisturizing regularly and protecting nails from harsh conditions can help mitigate these effects.

266: Nail Growth Can Be Affected by Medication

Certain medications, such as chemotherapy drugs, can affect nail growth and health. Side effects might include changes in nail color, texture, or growth patterns.

BRAIN POWER FACTS

267: Fascinating Facts About Your Mind

The Brain is the Most Complex Organ
The human brain is the most complex organ in the body, containing approximately 86 billion neurons. These neurons form an intricate network of connections that enable all cognitive functions.

268: Brain is About 75% Water

The brain is composed of about 75% water. This high water content is crucial for maintaining brain function and facilitating communication between neurons.

269: The Brain Consumes a Lot of Energy

Although the brain makes up only about 2% of your body weight, it consumes roughly 20% of the body's energy. This energy is used for maintaining neural activity and supporting cognitive processes.

270: Neuroplasticity

Neuroplasticity is the brain's ability to reorganize itself by forming new neural connections throughout life. This ability allows the brain to learn new skills, recover from injuries and adapt to new experiences,

271: Brain Cells Can Regenerate

Contrary to old beliefs, some brain cells can regenerate. The hippocampus, a region associated with memory and learning, can produce new neurons throughout a person's life, especially in response to learning and exercise.

272: The Left and Right Hemispheres

The brain is divided into two which is : the right and the left. Each hemisphere is responsible for different functions, with the left typically handling logical reasoning and language, and the right managing creativity and spatial awareness.

273: The Brain Processes Visual Information Quickly

The brain can process visual information extremely rapidly. It takes about 13 milliseconds for the brain to recognize an image, making it one of the fastest cognitive processes.

274: Dreams and the Brain

During the Rapid Eye Movement (REM) stage of sleep,dreams occur. During REM sleep, the brain is highly active, and it's believed that dreaming helps process emotions, memories, and problem-solving.

275: The Brain's Plasticity and Learning

Learning new skills or engaging in mental exercises can physically change the structure of the brain. This phenomenon, known as brain plasticity, supports the idea that continuous learning can enhance cognitive abilities.

276: The Brain's Capacity for Memory

The memory capacity of the human brain is enormous. It is calculated that the brain can save between 1 or 2.5 petabytes of data, equal to 1 million gigabytes.

277: Brain Waves and Mental States

The brain generates different types of brain waves (alpha, beta, theta, and delta) that correspond to various states of consciousness, such as relaxation, alertness, deep sleep, and meditation.

278: The Brain and Emotions

The limbic system, which includes the amygdala and hippocampus, plays a key role in regulating emotions and memory. This system helps process emotional responses and links them to memory formation.

279: Brain Size and Intelligence

Intelligence can not be determined by the size of the Brain. While larger brains may have more neurons and synaptic connections, intelligence is influenced by factors such as neural efficiency and connectivity.

280: The Brain Can Recognize Faces

The fusiform gyrus, a specialized area of the brain, is responsible for face recognition. This area helps individuals identify and remember faces, a crucial social skill.

281: Brain Connectivity and Intelligence

Research suggests that intelligence is related to the efficiency of brain connectivity. Highly intelligent individuals often have more efficient and organized neural networks, which facilitate faster and more effective processing.

282: The Brain's Sensory Integration

The brain combines data from several senses to provide a cohesive understanding of the outside environment. This multisensory integration allows individuals to experience a unified sensory experience, such as the taste and smell of food.

283: The Brain and Aging

As people age, the brain undergoes structural changes, including a decrease in brain volume and changes in connectivity. However, cognitive training and mental stimulation can help mitigate some of the effects of aging.

284: The Brain and Language

Language processing is primarily managed by the Broca's area and Wernicke's area in the brain. These regions are involved in speech production and comprehension, respectively.

285: Mirror Neurons and Empathy

Mirror neurons are a type of brain cell that responds to actions performed by others. These neurons play a role in empathy by allowing individuals to "mirror" and understand the emotions and actions of others.

286: The Brain's Role in Decision Making

The prefrontal cortex, located at the front of the brain, is crucial for decision-making, planning, and social behavior. It helps weigh options, consider consequences, and make informed choices.

287: The Brain and Pain Perception

The brain's perception of pain involves complex interactions between various brain regions, including the thalamus, somatosensory cortex, and limbic system. This system helps interpret and respond to painful stimuli.

288: The Brain's Natural Pain Relief

The brain produces natural painkillers called endorphins. These chemicals interact with the brain's opioid receptors to reduce the perception of pain and create feelings of euphoria.

289: The Brain's Capacity for Creativity

Creative thinking involves various brain regions, including the prefrontal cortex and the default mode network. These areas collaborate to generate novel ideas, solve problems, and engage in artistic expression.

290: The Brain and Memory Formation

Memory formation involves the hippocampus, which helps encode new information and consolidate it into long-term memory. The process of forming and retrieving memories is essential for learning and personal experience.

291: Brain-Body Connection

The brain communicates with the rest of the body through the nervous system, influencing various physiological processes. This brain-body connection plays a role in regulating functions like heart rate, digestion, and movement.

292: The Brain's Electrical Activity

The brain generates electrical activity that can be measured using an electroencephalogram (EEG). Different types of brain waves (alpha, beta, theta, and delta) correspond to various states of consciousness, such as relaxation, alertness, and deep sleep.

293: Brain Cells and Connectivity

The brain's neurons are highly interconnected, forming complex networks that facilitate communication. Each neuron can form thousands of synaptic connections with other neurons, allowing for intricate processing and information storage.

294: The Brain and Creativity

Creativity involves multiple brain regions, including the prefrontal cortex (for planning and problem-solving), the temporal lobes (for memory and perception), and the default mode network (associated with spontaneous thought and imagination).

295: The Brain's Plasticity

Neuroplasticity allows the brain to adapt and reorganize itself in response to experience, learning, and injury. This ability to change and reorganize is crucial for rehabilitation and learning new skills.

296: The Brain's "Power" Perception

The brain perceives power or effort differently based on context. For example, the sensation of exertion during physical activities is influenced by both sensory feedback and cognitive evaluation of effort.

297: The Role of the Thalamus

The thalamus acts as a relay station for sensory information, sending signals from sensory organs to the appropriate areas of the brain for processing. It plays an important role in motor control and sensory perception.

298: The Brain's Response to Music

Listening to music can activate multiple brain regions, including those involved in emotion, memory, and motor control. Music therapy can enhance cognitive function, improve mood, and aid in rehabilitation.

299: The Brain's Ability to Filter Information

The brain filters and prioritizes information based on relevance and importance. This selective attention allows individuals to focus on important tasks and ignore irrelevant stimuli.

300: Brainwaves and Learning

Different brainwave patterns are associated with different learning states. For instance, theta waves are linked to creativity and deep learning, while beta waves are associated with active problem-solving and concentration.

301:'The Brain's "Homeostatic" Regulation

The brain regulates internal balance and stability (homeostasis) by controlling body temperature, hunger, thirst, and circadian rhythms. This regulation helps maintain overall health and well-being.

302: The Impact of Stress on the Brain

Chronic stress can affect brain structure and function, particularly in regions like the hippocampus (involved in memory) and the prefrontal cortex (involved in decision-making). Managing stress through techniques like mindfulness can help mitigate these effects.

303:'The Brain's Development Over Time

The brain undergoes significant development throughout life. In childhood, the brain grows rapidly and forms connections, while in adolescence, it undergoes refinement and pruning. In adulthood, the brain continues to adapt and change based on experiences.

304: The Brain's "Rest" State

The default mode network (DMN) is active when the brain is at rest and not focused on the external environment. This network is involved in self-referential thinking, daydreaming, and internal reflection.

305: The Role of the Amygdala

The amygdala is important for processing emotions, especially fear and happiness. It helps regulate emotional responses and is involved in the formation of emotional memories.

306: Memory Formation and Recall

Memory formation involves encoding, storage, and retrieval processes. The hippocampus plays a key role in forming new memories, while the prefrontal cortex is involved in retrieving and organizing them.

307: The Brain's Adaptive Capacity

The brain's ability to adapt to new experiences and challenges is remarkable. For example, learning a new language or skill can create new neural pathways and strengthen existing connections.

308: The Brain and Sensory Integration

The brain integrates sensory information from different modalities (such as sight, sound, and touch) to create a cohesive perception of the environment. This integration allows for coordinated responses and accurate sensory experiences.

309: The Influence of Genetics on the Brain

Genetics play a significant role in brain development and function. Genetic variations can influence cognitive abilities, susceptibility to neurological disorders, and individual differences in brain structure and connectivity.

310:'Brain-Computer Interfaces

Advances in technology have led to the development of brain-computer interfaces (BCIs), which allow for direct communication between the brain and external devices. BCIs hold potential for applications in medical rehabilitation and assistive technologies.

311: The Brain and Sleep

Sleep is very important for a healthy brain, memory consolidation, and cognitive function. During sleep, the brain undergoes processes that help clear out waste products, reinforce learning, and regulate emotional responses.

312: The Brain's Capacity for Dual Tasking

The brain can perform multiple tasks simultaneously through a process known as dual-tasking. However, multitasking can sometimes reduce overall performance and efficiency, particularly when tasks compete for the same cognitive resources.

313: The Impact of Physical Exercise on the Brain

Regular physical exercise has been shown to enhance brain function, improve memory, and support mental health. Exercise promotes the release of neurochemicals and supports the growth of new neurons in the hippocampus.

314: The Role of the Prefrontal Cortex in Decision Making

The prefrontal cortex is crucial for executive functions, including planning, decision-making, and impulse control. It helps evaluate options, consider consequences, and make informed choices.

315: The Brain's Response to Novelty

Exposure to novel or unfamiliar stimuli can activate the brain's reward system and enhance learning. Novelty-seeking behaviors can stimulate curiosity and cognitive engagement.

HEART: THE ULTIMATE PUMP FACTS

316: The Heart's Mighty Output

The heart pumps around 2,000 gallons (7,570 liters) of blood through your body each day. This incredible feat is accomplished by beating about 100,000 times daily to ensure that oxygen and nutrients are delivered to every part of the body.

317: The Heart Never Rests

Unlike skeletal muscles, which need rest, the heart works continuously throughout your life. It's the only muscle that never tires, with its specialized cardiac muscle cells providing the endurance required for non-stop function.

318: The Size of the Heart
The size of the human heart is approximately that of a fist on average. It weighs between 8 and 12 ounces (250 to 350 grams), though the size can vary depending on a person's age, gender, and fitness level.

319: The Four Chambers of the Heart

The heart has four chambers: two atria (upper chambers) and two ventricles (lower chambers). The right side of the heart pumps deoxygenated blood to the lungs to get oxygen, while the left side pumps oxygen-rich blood to the rest of the body.

320: The Heart's Electrical System

The heart has its own electrical system, known as the cardiac conduction system, which regulates heartbeats. The sinoatrial (SA) node, often called the "natural pacemaker," sends electrical impulses that initiate each heartbeat.

321: The Heartbeat Sound

The familiar "lub-dub" sound of the heartbeat is caused by the opening and closing of the heart valves. The "lub" is the sound of the mitral and tricuspid valves closing, and the "dub" is the sound of the aortic and pulmonary valves closing.

322: Blood Flow in One Direction

The heart has four valves (mitral, tricuspid, aortic, and pulmonary) that ensure blood flows in one direction. These valves prevent the backflow of blood and help maintain efficient circulation throughout the body.

323: The Heart Beats Faster with Emotion

Emotions like excitement, stress, and fear can cause the heart to beat faster. This is due to the release of adrenaline, which prepares the body for action in situations of "fight or flight."

324: The Heart and Exercise

Regular exercise makes the heart muscle stronger and increases its pumping efficiency.Athletes often have a lower resting heart rate because their hearts can pump a larger volume of blood with each beat, reducing the need for a faster pulse.

325: The Heart's Blood Supply

The heart itself needs a constant supply of oxygen-rich blood, which is delivered through the coronary arteries. A heart attack (myocardial infarction) can result from blockage of these arteries.

326: The Heart and the Brain Connection

The heart and brain communicate constantly. The brain sends signals to regulate the heart rate, and in turn, the heart can influence brain function through the release of hormones like oxytocin, which is often called the "love hormone."

327: A Woman's Heart Beats Faster

Typically, a woman's heart beats quicker than a man's. A typical adult female heart beats about 78 times per minute, while a male heart beats around 70 times per minute.

328: The Heart and Fetal Development

A baby's heart starts beating at around three weeks after conception, well before many people even realize they're pregnant. By the time the baby is born, the heart will have already beaten millions of times.

329: Heart Cells Don't Regenerate Easily

Unlike many other cells in the body, heart muscle cells (cardiomyocytes) have limited ability to regenerate. This is why heart damage from conditions like heart attacks can have long-term effects.

330: The Heart and Blood Vessels

The heart pumps blood through an extensive network of blood vessels that, if stretched end-to-end, would cover approximately 60,000 miles (96,560 kilometers) , enough to circle the Earth more than twice!

331: The Heart and Laughter

Laughter really is good for your heart! Studies show that laughing can improve heart health by increasing blood flow and reducing stress. It also helps relax the blood vessels, contributing to better circulation.

332: Heart Rate and Age

As you age, your resting heart rate may decrease slightly, but your maximum heart rate during exercise decreases more significantly. To calculate your maximum heart rate, you can minus your age from 220.

333: Heart Attacks Can Happen Without Symptoms

Silent heart attacks can occur with little or no symptoms. These often go unnoticed but can still cause significant damage to the heart muscle. Regular check-ups and monitoring are key for early detection.

334: A Healthy Diet for a Healthy Heart

A heart-healthy diet rich in fruits, vegetables, whole grains, and healthy fats (like omega-3s from fish) can help reduce the risk of heart disease. Limiting sodium, trans fats, and added sugars is also crucial.

335: The Heart is a Symbol of Love

The heart has been used as a symbol of love and affection for centuries. This is partly due to the physical sensations we experience in the chest during strong emotions, reinforcing the idea that the heart is the center of feelings.

336: Heart Disease is the Leading Cause of Death Worldwide

Heart disease, including coronary artery disease, heart attacks, and heart failure, is the leading cause of death globally. However, lifestyle changes like regular exercise, a healthy diet, and avoiding smoking can significantly reduce the risk.

337: The Heart Rate Variability (HRV)

A heartbeat's fluctuation in duration is known as heart rate variability, or HRV. A higher HRV is often a sign of good cardiovascular health and indicates that the heart can adapt well to different stressors.

338: The First Successful Heart Transplant

The first successful human heart transplant was performed by Dr. Christiaan Barnard in South Africa in 1967. Since then, advancements in medicine have greatly improved the success rates and outcomes of heart transplants.

339: Heartbeats Begin in the Womb

A fetus's heart begins to beat as early as 18-21 days after conception. By the time the baby is born, the heart will have beaten about 54 million times.

340: Heart Disease and Genetics

While lifestyle factors play a major role, genetics can also influence heart health. People with a family history of heart disease should be more vigilant about regular check-ups and preventive measures.

LUNGS: BREATHING IN THE FACTS

341: The Lungs Are Massive

While they may seem compact, the surface area of the lungs is enormous. If unfolded, the lungs' surface area is about the size of a tennis court roughly 70 square meters! This large surface area is crucial for efficient gas exchange.

342: Two Lungs, Different Sizes

Humans have two lungs, but they aren't the same size. The right lung is larger and has three lobes, while the left lung has only two lobes to make room for the heart.

343: Breathing Rate

On average, an adult takes about 12 to 20 breaths per minute at rest. This adds up to approximately 17,000 to 30,000 breaths a day. Children tend to breathe faster, with rates of 20 to 30 breaths per minute.

344: Airways and Alveoli

The lungs contain a vast network of airways called bronchi and bronchioles, which lead to tiny sacs called alveoli. There are around 600 million alveoli in the lungs, and they are where oxygen and carbon dioxide are exchanged with the blood.

345: Gas Exchange in the Lungs

Gas exchange is the lungs' principal job.Oxygen from inhaled air passes into the bloodstream through the alveoli, and carbon dioxide, a waste product from metabolism, is expelled during exhalation.

346: Lungs and Buoyancy

The lungs help keep you afloat in water. Their capacity to hold air means that the lungs act like internal flotation devices, which is why humans naturally float in water, especially when lying on their backs.

347: The Role of the Diaphragm

The muscle at the base of the lungs is called the diaphragm, and it has a dome shape. When you breathe in, it flattens and compresses, creating a vacuum that draws air into your lungs. The diaphragm relaxes and pushes air out during exhalation.

348: Lungs and Blood

The lungs are a key player in blood oxygenation. Every minute, the lungs receive approximately 5 liters (1.3 gallons) of blood, which is then oxygenated and sent back into circulation to fuel the body's organs and tissues.

349: Mucus Production

The lungs produce mucus to trap dust, microbes, and other harmful particles inhaled from the environment. Tiny hair-like structures called cilia then move the mucus up to the throat, where it can be swallowed or coughed out.

350: Breathing and Brain Function

The brainstem controls the automatic process of breathing, adjusting your breathing rate based on your body's oxygen needs and carbon dioxide levels. This is why you breathe faster when exercising or when your body requires more oxygen.

351: Lung Capacity and Exercise

Regular physical exercise can increase lung capacity, improving the efficiency of oxygen exchange. Athletes and those who regularly engage in cardiovascular exercise often have better lung function and can take deeper, more efficient breaths.

352:The Lungs Are Self-Cleaning

The lungs have a remarkable ability to clean themselves. When a person quits smoking, for example, the lungs begin to repair and cleanse themselves, gradually expelling tar and other harmful substances.

353: Lung Diseases

Lung cancer, pneumonia, asthma, and chronic obstructive pulmonary disease (COPD) are among the common lung ailments. Maintaining lung health through avoiding pollutants, not smoking, and regular exercise is crucial to preventing these diseases.

354: Breathing Through the Nose vs. Mouth

Breathing through the nose is better for lung health because the nasal passages filter, humidify, and warm the air before it reaches the lungs. Mouth breathing can lead to dry airways and reduced filtration of harmful particles.

355: Lung Capacity Declines With Age

As you age, lung capacity naturally decreases. After the age of 30, the lungs' elasticity diminishes, and the muscles used for breathing weaken slightly, which can reduce overall lung function.

356: The Lungs Play a Role in Speech

The lungs are essential for speech. Air from the lungs passes through the vocal cords in the larynx (voice box), allowing for sound production. The force and control of exhaled air impact the volume and pitch of your voice.

357: Oxygen Usage

The lungs absorb about 21% of the oxygen in the air you inhale, but only about 16% of that oxygen is used by the body. The rest is exhaled, which is why rescue breathing (like CPR) can supply enough oxygen to keep someone alive.

358: Lung Health and Pollution

Exposure to air pollution can severely impact lung health, causing conditions like asthma and bronchitis. The World Health Organization estimates that air pollution contributes to around 7 million premature deaths each year, many related to lung conditions.

359: Lungs and Stress

Stress can alter your breathing patterns, often causing shallow, rapid breaths. Deep, diaphragmatic breathing (using the diaphragm) is a relaxation technique that can reduce stress and promote lung health.

360: Your Lungs and Altitude

At high altitudes, the air contains less oxygen, which forces your lungs to work harder to oxygenate the blood. Over time, your body adapts by producing more red blood cells to compensate for the lower oxygen levels.

361: Sneezing Clears the Airways

Sneezing is a reflex designed to clear irritants from the respiratory system. When your nasal passages detect an irritant, the lungs forcefully expel air at speeds up to 100 miles per hour to remove it.

362: Breath Holding

Over 24 minutes is the world record for the longest breath hold! While most people can only hold their breath for about 30 seconds to 2 minutes, training and conditioning can improve this ability.

363: Lung Transplants

In 1963, the first lung transplant operation was completed successfully. Since then, advancements in medical technology have made lung transplants a viable treatment for people with severe lung diseases.

364: Lung Regeneration

While the lungs don't regenerate as easily as other organs, some parts of the lungs can repair themselves. For example, lung tissue can partially recover from damage caused by smoking or pollution if the exposure is removed.

365: Sleep and Lung Health

Sleep is important for lung health. Poor sleep can weaken your immune system, making you more susceptible to respiratory infections. Additionally, conditions like sleep apnea, which affects breathing during sleep, can strain the lungs and heart.

DIGESTIVE SYSTEM: THE JOURNEY OF YOUR FOOD FACTS

366: Digestion Begins in the Mouth

Digestion starts before you even swallow! The sight, smell, and even thought of food can trigger saliva production, which contains enzymes that begin breaking down carbohydrates while you chew.

367: The Esophagus: A Food Conveyor

Once you swallow, food travels down the esophagus through a series of muscle contractions called peristalsis. This conveyor belt-like movement pushes food into the stomach in just a few seconds, no matter your body's position.

368: The Stomach Is a Churning Machine

The stomach acts as a powerful blender, churning food with digestive juices, including hydrochloric acid and enzymes, to break it down into a thick liquid called chyme. The acid is so strong it can dissolve metal, but the stomach's mucus lining protects it from self-digestion.

369: Small Intestine: Where Absorption Happens

The majority of nutrients from meals enter the circulation in the small intestine. Measuring about 20 feet long, this organ has tiny finger-like projections called villi, which increase surface area to absorb nutrients efficiently.

370: The Liver's Vital Role

The liver produces bile, a digestive fluid stored in the gallbladder and released into the small intestine to help digest fats. The liver also plays a crucial role in metabolizing nutrients, detoxifying harmful substances, and storing vitamins and minerals.

371: Food Travels About 30 Feet Through the Digestive Tract

From mouth to anus, food travels a distance of roughly 30 feet (9 meters) through the entire digestive system. Each section has a specific function, working together to process food, extract nutrients, and expel waste.

372: The Large Intestine: Water Absorption

After nutrients are absorbed in the small intestine, the remaining material enters the large intestine (colon), which is about 5 feet long. Here, water and electrolytes are absorbed, and the leftover waste is prepared for elimination.

373: The Role of Gut Bacteria

Your digestive system is home to trillions of bacteria, known as the gut microbiome. These bacteria aid in breaking down food, producing vitamins like B12 and K, and maintaining a healthy immune system. They also play a role in mood regulation through the gut-brain connection.

374: The Stomach Doesn't Do Most of the Digesting

Contrary to popular belief, the stomach is not where most digestion occurs. While it breaks down food with acid and enzymes, most digestion and nutrient absorption take place in the small intestine.

375: You Produce 1 to 2 Quarts of Stomach Acid Daily

Your stomach produces 1 to 2 quarts of acid every day to break down food. Despite its strength, the stomach's mucous lining protects the organ from the corrosive acid.

376: The Digestive System Is Like a Second Brain

The gut is often referred to as the "second brain" because of the enteric nervous system, a complex network of neurons in the gutter that operates independently of the central nervous system. This system controls digestion and can influence emotions and stress levels.

377: The Digestive Process Takes Time

The transit time of food through the stomach and small intestine is around 6 to 8 hours. It can take another 12 to 24 hours for the food to pass through the large intestine, depending on factors like the type of food consumed and hydration levels.

378: Your Digestive System Never Rests

Even when you're asleep, your digestive system keeps working. While the process slows down during rest, it continues to break down food and absorb nutrients, allowing your body to recover and rejuvenate overnight.

379: Chewing Your Food Thoroughly Aids Digestion

The more you chew, the easier it is for your stomach and intestines to break down the food. Chewing properly increases saliva production, which contains enzymes that help digest carbohydrates and fats early in the process.

380: The Stomach Can Stretch

Your stomach can hold about 1 liter of food and liquid, but it can expand to hold up to 4 liters! This flexibility allows the stomach to accommodate larger meals, but overeating can cause discomfort.

381: Gurgling Sounds in the Stomach

Those familiar gurgling sounds your stomach makes, known as borborygmi, are caused by gas and fluid moving through the intestines. These sounds occur even when you're not hungry, as your digestive system remains active.

382: Food Travels Through the Intestines in 24 to 72 Hours

From the moment you eat, it typically takes between 24 and 72 hours for food to be fully digested and eliminated as waste. The exact time depends on factors such as metabolism, diet, and hydration.

383: Farting Is a Normal Part of Digestion

The average person passes gas around 14 to 23 times a day. This is the result of bacteria in the intestines breaking down certain foods and releasing gas. Foods high in fiber, such as beans and lentils, are common culprits.

384: The Appendix May Have a Function After All

Long thought to be a vestigial organ, recent research suggests that the appendix may play a role in storing good bacteria and supporting immune function. While not essential for survival, it may have a purpose in maintaining gut health.

385: Spicy Foods Don't Actually Cause Ulcers

Contrary to popular belief, spicy foods are not responsible for causing ulcers. Most ulcers are caused by infections with the bacteria Helicobacter pylori or the overuse of nonsteroidal anti-inflammatory drugs (NSAIDs), not by diet.

386: The Liver Can Regenerate

The only internal organ capable of self-regeneration is the liver.
Even if up to 70% of the liver is damaged or removed, it can grow back to its original size within a few months, making it vital for detoxifying the body.

387: Fiber is Essential for Digestion

Fiber helps keep the digestive system running smoothly by adding bulk to stools and promoting regular bowel movements. Foods like fruits, vegetables, whole grains, and legumes are rich in fiber and are key to digestive health.

388: The Stomach Replace Its Lining Every Few Days

The stomach's lining is replaced every three to four days to protect it from being damaged by its own acid. Without this constant renewal, the stomach's tissues would be eroded by the digestive fluids.

389: The Gallbladder's Role in Digestion

The liver produces bile, which the gallbladder stores and then distributes into the small intestine to aid with fat digestion. While the gallbladder is useful, it's not essential—people can live without it, although fat digestion may become less efficient.

390: Swallowing Air Causes Bloating

Swallowing air while eating or drinking too quickly can lead to bloating and gas. Chewing slowly, drinking less carbonated beverages, and avoiding talking while eating can help reduce this issue.

LIVER: DETOX FACTS YOU SHOULD KNOW

391: Liver: The Body's Chemical Processing Plant

Your Liver Filters Everything You Consume.
The liver is the body's largest internal organ, weighing about 3 pounds. It processes nutrients from food and drinks, filters toxins from the blood, and helps the body absorb essential vitamins and minerals.

392: The Liver Has Over 500 Functions

The liver performs more than 500 vital functions, including breaking down fats, producing proteins needed for blood clotting, and storing glycogen for energy. It also helps regulate hormone levels and processes medications.

393: Alcohol and the Liver

About one standard drink can be metabolized by the liver in an hour. Excessive alcohol consumption can overwhelm the liver, leading to the accumulation of fat, inflammation, and scarring, which can result in liver disease or cirrhosis.

394: Liver Regeneration Is Remarkable

The liver is remarkable in its capacity for self-regeneration. If up to 70% of the liver is damaged or removed, the remaining portion can grow back to its original size within months, making it one of the most resilient organs in the body.

395: The Liver Produces Bile

The liver creates and stores bile, a digesting fluid, in the gallbladder.
It helps break down fats in the small intestine, aiding in digestion. Bile also carries waste products like bilirubin out of the body.

396: Fatty Liver Disease Is Common

Non-alcoholic fatty liver disease (NAFLD) is the most common liver disorder, affecting around 25% of people worldwide. It's caused by the accumulation of fat in the liver, often linked to obesity, diabetes, and poor diet.

397: The Liver Neutralizes Toxins

The liver breaks down harmful substances like alcohol, drugs, and environmental toxins into less harmful compounds that can be safely excreted from the body. It converts ammonia, a byproduct of protein metabolism, into urea, which the kidneys then filter out.

398: Liver and Blood Sugar Control

The liver plays a critical role in regulating blood sugar levels. It stores glucose as glycogen and releases it when the body needs energy, ensuring that blood sugar levels remain stable throughout the day.

399: Medications and the Liver

Many medications, including over-the-counter drugs like acetaminophen (Tylenol), are processed by the liver. Taking too much of these medications can damage the liver, leading to acute liver failure.

400: Jaundice: A Sign of Liver Trouble

Jaundice occurs when the liver fails to process bilirubin, a yellow pigment produced by the breakdown of red blood cells. This leads to yellowing of the skin and eyes and is often a sign of liver disease or dysfunction.

KIDNEYS: THE BODY'S FILTRATION SYSTEM FACTS

401: Kidneys Filter About 50 Gallons of Blood Daily

The kidneys are highly efficient filtration organs. They filter your blood about 40 times a day, removing waste products and excess water to form urine. Each kidney contains around 1 million tiny filtering units called nephrons.

402: Kidneys Regulate Blood Pressure

Renin, a hormone that the kidneys generate, aids in blood pressure regulation. When blood pressure is too low, the kidneys release renin, triggering a series of reactions that cause blood vessels to constrict and raise pressure.

403: Hydration and Kidney Function

Drinking enough water is crucial for kidney health. Dehydration reduces kidney function, leading to concentrated urine and a higher risk of kidney stones and infections. Staying hydrated helps the kidneys flush out toxins effectively.

404: The Kidneys Control Electrolyte Balance

The kidneys maintain the balance of essential electrolytes, including sodium, potassium, and calcium, which are vital for muscle and nerve function. They filter out excess amounts of these minerals and retain what the body needs.

405: Kidney Stones: A Painful Problem

Kidney stones form when minerals like calcium and oxalate crystallize in the kidneys. These hard deposits can cause severe pain as they move through the urinary tract. Staying hydrated can help prevent their formation.

406: Kidneys and Red Blood Cell Production

Erythropoietin is a hormone that the kidneys make that causes the bone marrow to create red blood cells.

This is important for maintaining adequate oxygen levels in the blood, especially in response to low oxygen environments.

407: Kidneys Remove Urea

One waste product that is produced when proteins break down is urea. The kidneys remove urea from the blood and eliminate it through urine, Elevated levels of urea can indicate kidney problems or dehydration.

408: High Blood Pressure Can Damage the Kidneys

Hypertension (high blood pressure) can damage the blood vessels in the kidneys, reducing their ability to filter blood. Chronic kidney disease often develops as a result of long-term uncontrolled hypertension.

409: The Kidneys Regulate Acid-Base Balance

By reabsorbing bicarbonate from urine and excreting hydrogen ions, the kidneys aid in maintaining the pH equilibrium of the body. This process ensures that the body maintains a stable internal environment, preventing dangerous shifts in acidity.

410: Dialysis Replaces Kidney Function

When the kidneys are unable to filter blood effectively due to kidney failure, dialysis is used to perform this function. Hemodialysis involves a machine that cleans the blood outside the body, while peritoneal dialysis uses the lining of the abdomen to filter waste.

STOMACH FACTS

411: Stomach Acid Can Dissolve materials

The hydrochloric acid (HCl) in the stomach is so strong it could dissolve materials like bone and teeth. With a pH of around 1-2, it's almost as acidic as battery acid, but the stomach's protective lining keeps it from damaging itself.

412: Your Stomach Gets a New Lining Every Few Days

To protect itself from its own harsh acid, the stomach regenerates its lining every 3 to 4 days. Without this constant renewal, the stomach would essentially digest itself.

413: The Stomach Isn't Where Most Digestion Happens

While the stomach plays a crucial role in breaking down food with acid and enzymes, most digestion and nutrient absorption happens in the small intestine. The stomach mainly churns food into a semi-liquid substance called chyme.

414: It Takes 2-3 Hours for Your Stomach to Empty

After a meal, it takes about 2 to 3 hours for the stomach to break down food and pass it on to the small intestine. Factors like the type of food, stress levels, and hydration can affect how long digestion takes.

415: The Stomach Can Expand Significantly

When empty, the stomach holds about 50 milliliters (1.7 ounces), but after a meal, it can expand to hold 1 to 1.5 liters (up to 50 ounces) of food and liquid. In extreme cases, it can expand even further.

416: The "Growling" Sound Comes From the Stomach

Stomach growling, known as borborygmi, is caused by gas and fluid moving through the digestive system. Even when you're not eating, the stomach contracts regularly, which can cause these noises.

417: The Stomach Has Its Own "Brain"

The stomach and digestive system are controlled by the enteric nervous system, often called the "second brain." It operates independently of the central nervous system and plays a big role in regulating digestion.

418: The Stomach Doesn't Just Digest Food

Besides breaking down food, the stomach also helps absorb some essential nutrients, like vitamin B12, which is crucial for nerve function and the production of red blood cells. The stomach releases a protein called intrinsic factor that's needed for B12 absorption.

419: The Stomach Produces About 3 Liters of Gastric Juice Daily

The stomach secretes 2 to 3 liters of gastric juice each day, a mixture of hydrochloric acid, digestive enzymes, and mucus, which aids in breaking down food into nutrients that the body can absorb.

420:'Stomach Ulcers Aren't Caused by Spicy Foods

Contrary to popular belief, spicy foods don't cause ulcers. Most ulcers are caused by a bacterium called Helicobacter pylori or by long-term use of anti-inflammatory drugs like ibuprofen. Spicy foods might aggravate existing ulcers but aren't usually the root cause.

421: The Stomach Changes Shape as You Move

The stomach is a flexible organ, constantly changing shape depending on your position (lying down, standing up, etc.) and the amount of food inside it. It can shift around, especially during activities like exercise.

422: Stomach Cells Can Produce Hormones

In addition to digestive enzymes, the stomach produces hormones like ghrelin, also known as the "hunger hormone." Ghrelin signals your brain when it's time to eat, making you feel hungry.

423: Food Doesn't Stay in the Stomach for Long

Carbohydrates like bread and pasta move quickly through the stomach, while fats take the longest to digest. On average, food stays in the stomach for about 2 to 4 hours before moving into the small intestine.

424: Acid Reflux Is Caused by a Weak Valve

Acid reflux occurs when the lower esophageal sphincter (LES), the valve between the esophagus and stomach, doesn't close properly. This allows stomach acid to rise into the esophagus, causing a burning sensation, commonly known as heartburn.

425: Your Stomach Can Function Without Food for Days

The stomach can contract and release enzymes for days even if no food is ingested. During fasting or periods without food, the body switches to burning stored fat for energy, and the stomach continues to release digestive juices in anticipation of food.

426: The Stomach Does Not Directly "Feel" Pain

While the stomach can produce discomfort through indigestion or ulcers, it doesn't feel pain in the same way the skin does. Pain in the stomach is typically related to the brain by surrounding nerves, which is why it sometimes feels like a dull ache or pressure rather than sharp pain.

INTESTINES FACTS

427: Your Small Intestine Is Really Long

Despite its name, the small intestine is about 20 feet long (6 meters), making it much longer than the large intestine. Its "small" name comes from its diameter, which is about 1 inch (2.5 cm), compared to the large intestine's 3 inches (7.5 cm).

428: Surface Area of the Small Intestine Is Huge

If you spread out the inner lining of the small intestine, it would cover about 2,700 square feet (250 square meters) the size of a tennis court! This large surface area, created by villi and microvilli (tiny hair-like projections), helps absorb nutrients more efficiently.

429: Food Travels Fast Through the Small Intestine

After food leaves the stomach, it travels through the small intestine in about 3 to 6 hours. During this time, digestive enzymes break down food, and nutrients are absorbed into the bloodstream.

430: The Large Intestine Is Much Shorter

The large intestine, also known as the colon, is about 5 feet long (1.5 meters). Its main function is to absorb water and electrolytes, as well as store waste before it's eliminated from the body.

431: Most Gut Bacteria Live in the Large Intestine

The large intestine is home to trillions of bacteria, known as the gut microbiome. These bacteria play a crucial role in digesting fiber, producing vitamins like vitamin K, and keeping harmful bacteria in check.

432: The Small Intestine Does Most of the Digestive Work

While the stomach starts breaking down food, 90% of digestion and nutrient absorption happens in the small intestine. Carbohydrates, proteins, fats, vitamins, and minerals are all absorbed here with the help of digestive enzymes and bile.

433: The Large Intestine Absorbs a Lot of Water

The large intestine absorbs about a quart (or liter) of water every day. This process turns the watery waste from digestion into solid stool before it's excreted.

434: Your Intestines Move Food with Muscular Waves

The intestines use a process called peristalsis, which involves rhythmic contractions of the smooth muscles lining the digestive tract. This moves food and waste along the digestive system in a wave-like motion.

435: The Appendix Might Not Be Useless After All

Long thought to be a vestigial organ with no purpose, recent studies suggest that the appendix may serve as a "safe house" for beneficial bacteria, helping the body recover gut bacteria after infections.

436: Your Gut Is Linked to Your Brain

The enteric nervous system, often called the "second brain," governs your digestive system. This network of neurons communicates directly with your brain, which is why stress or anxiety can cause stomach aches or digestive issues.

437: Intestines Make Their Own Sounds

The intestines produce gurgling noises (borborygmi) as gas and fluids move through them. These sounds are normal and can happen even when you're not hungry, as the intestines are always working.

438: It Takes About 24 to 72 Hours for Food to Pass Through the Whole System

From the time you eat until waste exits your body, it takes 24 to 72 hours. This timeline depends on factors like the type of food, hydration, and your individual digestive health.

439: Your Intestines Produce "Feel-Good" Chemicals

Approximately 95% of the body's serotonin, a neurotransmitter important for mood control, sleep, and digestion, is produced in the stomach.
This highlights the strong connection between your gut and mental health.

440: The Small Intestine Breaks Down Complex Sugars

Enzymes in the small intestine break down complex carbohydrates (like starches) into simple sugars. These sugars are then absorbed into the bloodstream, providing the body with energy.

441: The Large Intestine and Gas Production

Bacteria in the large intestine ferment undigested food, producing gasses like methane and hydrogen. On average, humans pass gas 14 to 23 times per day—this is a natural part of digestion!

442: The Colon Can Store Waste for Days

While the entire digestion process usually takes less than a day, the large intestine can store waste for longer periods, especially if you're constipated. The colon extracts water from waste, turning it into solid stool for elimination.

443: Fiber Is the Intestines' Best Friend

Fiber, found in fruits, vegetables, and whole grains, is crucial for maintaining intestinal health. It helps keep bowel movements regular by adding bulk to stool and feeds the beneficial bacteria in the large intestine.

444: The Small Intestine Has a Protective Lining

The inner surface of the small intestine is lined with mucus, protecting it from being damaged by stomach acid. This mucus also aids in the movement of food through the digestive tract.

445: Your Intestines Are Always Active

Even when you're asleep, your intestines are still busy digesting food. The body's digestive processes slow down at night, but peristalsis and nutrient absorption continue throughout the day and night.

446: You Produce 1 to 2 Liters of Intestinal Gas Per Day

The bacteria in your intestines break down undigested food, producing gas as a byproduct. On average, the intestines produce about 1 to 2 liters of gas per day, which is released naturally throughout the day.

THE IMMUNE SYSTEM: YOUR BODY'S DEFENDERS

447: The Immune System Is Made Up of Different Components

The immune system includes a range of components such as white blood cells, antibodies, complement proteins, and lymphatic organs (like the spleen and lymph nodes) that work together to protect the body from infections and diseases.

448: White Blood Cells Are the Immune System's Frontline Soldiers

The main immune system cells are called leukocytes, or white blood cells. They come in various types, including neutrophils, lymphocytes (T cells and B cells), and monocytes, each with specific roles in identifying and attacking pathogens.

449: The Immune System Can Recognize Millions of Pathogens

The immune system has the remarkable ability to recognize and respond to potentially millions of different pathogens, thanks to its diverse array of immune cells and receptors that can identify unique molecules on the surface of viruses, bacteria, and other invaders.

450: Antibodies Are Specific to Each Pathogen

Antibodies, also known as immunoglobulins, are proteins produced by B cells that bind specifically to antigens on pathogens.

451: The Immune System Has Memory

After an initial exposure to a pathogen, the immune system creates memory cells that remember how to recognize and fight that specific pathogen. This is why vaccines and prior infections often provide long-lasting protection against certain diseases.

452: The Thymus Gland Trains T Cells

The thymus gland, located behind the sternum, is where T cells mature and learn to distinguish between the body's own cells and foreign invaders. This process is crucial for preventing autoimmune diseases, where the immune system attacks its own tissues.

453: The Spleen Filters Blood and Manages Immune Responses

The spleen, located in the upper left abdomen, filters blood to remove old or damaged red blood cells and pathogens. It also helps activate immune responses by producing and storing immune cells.

454: Lymph Nodes Are Surveillance Centers

Lymph nodes are small, bean-shaped structures scattered throughout the body that filter lymph fluid, trapping pathogens and providing a site for immune cells to interact and mount a response.

455: The Immune System Is Affected by Stress

Chronic stress can impair immune function by disrupting the balance of immune cells and hormones, making the body more susceptible to infections and slowing down the recovery process.

456: Gut Health Is Linked to Immune Function

The gut-associated lymphoid tissue (GALT) plays a key role in detecting pathogens and maintaining immune tolerance to harmless substances, such as food and beneficial bacteria.

457: The Immune System Can Sometimes Overreact

Allergies occur when the immune system overreacts to harmless substances, such as pollen or certain foods, treating them as threats and causing symptoms like itching, swelling, and sneezing.

458: Autoimmune Diseases Occur When the Immune System Misfires

This occurs when the immune system mistakenly attacks the body's own tissues. Examples include multiple sclerosis, rheumatoid arthritis, and lupus.

These conditions can cause inflammation and damage to various organs.

459: The Immune System Can Be Compromised by Certain Conditions

Conditions like HIV/AIDS, which attack immune cells directly, and other immunodeficiencies can severely impair the body's ability to fight infections. People become more vulnerable to opportunistic infections and illnesses as a result.

460: The Skin and Mucous Membranes Are the First Line of Defense

The skin and mucous membranes (in the nose, mouth, and other body openings) act as physical barriers to prevent pathogens from entering the body. They also produce antimicrobial substances that help kill or inhibit the growth of microorganisms.

461: Fevers Are a Sign of Immune Response

A fever is a common response to infection where the body raises its temperature to help fight off pathogens. Higher temperatures can inhibit the growth of some bacteria and enhance the performance of immune cells.

462: Immunity Can Be Acquired Naturally or Artificially

Immunity can be acquired through natural infection or artificially through vaccines. Vaccines stimulate the immune system to produce memory cells without causing the disease, providing protection against future infections.

463: Immune System Cells Communicate Through Signals

Immune cells communicate with each other using chemical signals called cytokines. These signals help coordinate the immune response by regulating the activity and growth of immune cells and influencing inflammation.

464: The Immune System Continues to Evolve

The immune system is constantly adapting to new threats. It evolves through processes like somatic hypermutation and clonal selection, which help it keep up with evolving pathogens and emerging diseases.

465: Healthy Lifestyle Supports Immune Function

A balanced diet, regular exercise, adequate sleep, and good hygiene practices all contribute to a well-functioning immune system. These lifestyle factors help maintain the body's ability to respond effectively to infections and diseases

CIRCULATORY SYSTEM: AMAZING BLOOD FACTS

466: Your Body Contains About 1.5 Gallons of Blood

The average adult has about 1.2 to 1.5 gallons (4.5 to 5.7 liters) of blood, which makes up about 7-8% of your total body weight. This blood circulates through your body, delivering oxygen and nutrients to cells and removing waste.

467: Blood Travels a Long Distance Every Day

If you could stretch out all your blood vessels, they would measure about 60,000 miles (96,500 kilometers) long!That would take it more than twice around the planet. Blood travels this vast distance every day through your circulatory system.

468: Blood Makes a Complete Circuit in Less Than a Minute

In just 20 seconds, blood can circulate through the entire body. The heart pumps blood at an incredible speed, ensuring that oxygen, nutrients, and waste are continuously exchanged in the cells.

469: Red Blood Cells Have a Lifespan of 120 Days

Red blood cells (RBCs), which are responsible for carrying oxygen, live for about 120 days before they are replaced. The body constantly produces new red blood cells in the bone marrow to maintain a healthy supply.

470: Blood Is Made Up of Four Key Components

Red blood cells, white blood cells, platelets, and plasma make up blood.

Plasma, which makes up about 55% of your blood, is mostly water but also contains proteins, hormones, and nutrients.

471: Your Heart Pumps About 2,000 Gallons of Blood a Day

The heart is a powerful muscle that pumps about 2,000 gallons (7,570 liters) of blood every day. It beats approximately 100,000 times per day, working around the clock to keep blood flowing through your body.

472: Blood Is Red Because of Hemoglobin

Hemoglobin, the protein in red blood cells that binds to oxygen, contains iron, which gives blood its bright red color when oxygenated. When blood lacks oxygen, it appears darker or bluish, which is why veins sometimes look blue under the skin.

473: There Are 8 Main Blood Types

Human blood is classified into four main blood types: A, B, AB, and O, which can be either positive or negative, making eight main blood types in total. Your blood type is determined by the presence of specific antigens on your red blood cells.

474: White Blood Cells Are Your Body's Defense Force

Your immune system's white blood cells (WBCs) are an essential component.They fight infections by attacking viruses, bacteria, and other foreign invaders. Unlike red blood cells, which are produced continuously, white blood cells are created on demand.

475: Platelets Help Blood Clot

Tiny cell fragments called platelets are essential for blood coagulation.

When you get a cut, platelets gather at the injury site and form a clot to stop bleeding. Without platelets, even a small cut could result in significant blood loss.

476: Blood Transports Oxygen, Nutrients, and Waste

Blood not only carries oxygen from the lungs to the rest of the body, but it also delivers nutrients from the digestive system and removes waste products like carbon dioxide and urea for excretion.

477: The Spleen Filters and Recycles Blood

The spleen acts as a blood filter, removing old or damaged red blood cells from circulation. It also stores white blood cells and helps fight infections by producing antibodies.

478: Blood Volume Can Increase During Pregnancy

During pregnancy, a woman's blood volume increases by up to 50% to support the growing fetus. This additional blood helps supply oxygen and nutrients to the baby and supports the placenta.

479: You Can Lose a Lot of Blood Before It's Dangerous

The human body can lose up to 15% of its total blood volume without experiencing serious health issues. However, losing more than 40% can lead to shock, and in extreme cases, can be life-threatening without immediate medical intervention.

480: The Blood Cells Are Constantly Renewed

Every second, your body produces about 2 million new red blood cells to replace those that are lost. This constant renewal ensures that your body always has a fresh supply of oxygen-carrying cells.

481: Blood Can Carry Information About Your Health

Blood tests can reveal a lot about your health, from measuring sugar levels (to check for diabetes) to identifying infections and determining your cholesterol levels. Doctors rely on blood samples to diagnose and monitor a wide variety of conditions.

482: The First Blood Transfusion Was in the 1600s

The first documented blood transfusion took place in the 1660s by French physician Jean-Baptiste Denis. He transfused blood from animals into humans, though these early experiments were largely unsuccessful until the discovery of blood types in the early 20th century.

483: The Average Person Donates About a Pint of Blood

When you donate blood, you typically give about 1 pint (0.47 liters) of blood, which is around 10% of your total blood volume. The body can replace this lost blood within a few days, making blood donation a safe and lifesaving practice.

484: The Liver Produces Most of the Blood's Plasma Proteins

The liver produces important proteins found in blood plasma, including albumin and clotting factors. These proteins help maintain blood pressure and are essential for blood clotting and healing.

485: Your Blood Pressure Is Essential for Circulation

Blood pressure, the force exerted by circulating blood on the walls of blood vessels, ensures that blood moves efficiently through the body. Normal blood pressure is crucial for delivering oxygen and nutrients to tissues and organs.

SPINE: SUPPORT AND MOVEMENT

486: The Spine Has 33 Vertebrae

The human spine is made up of 33 individual bones called vertebrae, which are stacked on top of each other. These vertebrae are divided into five regions: cervical (neck), thoracic (upper back), lumbar (lower back), sacral, and coccygeal (tailbone).

487:'The Spine Provides Both Strength and Flexibility

The spine is designed to support the body's weight and provide flexibility for movement. It acts as a central support structure, allowing you to stand upright, bend, twist, and move in many directions.

488: Spinal Discs Act as Shock Absorbers

Between each vertebra is a soft, cushion-like structure called an intervertebral disc. These discs absorb shock, reduce friction, and allow the spine to flex and move smoothly without damaging the bones.

489: The Spinal Cord Runs Through the Spine

The spinal cord, a bundle of nerves that connects the brain to the rest of the body, runs through a hollow space in the middle of the spine. This is why the spine is so important—it not only supports movement but also protects this vital part of the nervous system.

490: The Spine's Shape Resembles an "S"

The spine has a natural S-shaped curve, which helps distribute the weight of the body evenly and provides balance. This curvature helps reduce the impact from activities like walking, running, and lifting.

491: The Cervical Spine Supports Your Head

The cervical spine consists of the top seven vertebrae (C1–C7) and is responsible for supporting the weight of your head, which weighs around 10-12 pounds (4.5–5.5 kg). It also allows for a wide range of head movements.

492: The Lumbar Spine Bears Most of the Body's Weight

The lumbar region, consisting of five vertebrae (L1–L5), is located in the lower back and bears most of the body's weight. This is why this area is most prone to injury, especially during heavy lifting or repetitive movements.

493: You Shrink a Little Every Day

Throughout the day, the intervertebral discs lose water due to the pressure exerted on them while standing or sitting. As a result, you can lose up to 1 centimeter (0.4 inches) in height by the end of the day. The discs rehydrate while you sleep, restoring your height.

494: The Sacrum and Coccyx Are Fused Vertebrae

The sacrum and coccyx (tailbone) are made up of fused vertebrae. The sacrum is a triangular bone located at the base of the spine, connecting the spine to the pelvis, while the coccyx is the small bone at the very bottom of the spine.

495: The Spine Helps with Posture

Good posture relies on a healthy spine. Keeping your spine properly aligned while standing, sitting, and moving helps reduce strain on the muscles and ligaments, preventing back pain and injury.

496: Spinal Nerves Control Movement and Sensation

31 pairs of spinal nerves branch out from the spinal cord, exiting through openings between the vertebrae. These nerves control movement, sensation, and reflexes throughout the body, from your arms and legs to your internal organs.

497: Herniated Discs Can Cause Nerve Pain

A herniated disc occurs when the soft inner material of a disc pushes through its outer layer, often pressing on nearby nerves. This can cause pain, numbness, or weakness in the back, legs, or arms, depending on the location of the herniation.

498: The Spine Is Affected by Aging

As we age, the spine undergoes changes, such as degenerative disc disease, where the discs between the vertebrae lose hydration and become less flexible. This can lead to stiffness, pain, and reduced mobility over time.

499: Scoliosis Is a Curvature of the Spine

Scoliosis is a condition where the spine curves sideways in an abnormal "C" or "S" shape. It can range from mild to severe and often develops during adolescence, though it can occur at any age.

500:Yoga and Stretching Benefit the Spine

Regular stretching and exercises like yoga help keep the spine flexible, reduce tension in the surrounding muscles, and maintain proper alignment. These activities also strengthen the core muscles, which support the spine and improve posture.

501: Your Spine Supports Your Nervous System

The spine plays a critical role in supporting your nervous system. Spinal adjustments or manipulations, such as those used in chiropractic care, are often used to help relieve pressure on spinal nerves and improve overall health and function.

502: Back Pain Is One of the Most Common Medical Problems

About 80% of adults experience back pain at some point in their lives. Common causes include poor posture, muscle strain, herniated discs, and arthritis. Keeping the spine healthy through exercise, proper lifting techniques, and maintaining a healthy weight can help prevent back pain.

RED BLOOD CELLS: OXYGEN'S JOURNEY

503: Red Blood Cells Are Oxygen's Transport System

Red blood cells (RBCs) are responsible for carrying oxygen from the lungs to every cell in the body. They achieve this through hemoglobin, a protein that binds to oxygen molecules.

504: Hemoglobin Turns Blood Red

The iron in hemoglobin gives blood its bright red color when it binds with oxygen. When red blood cells release oxygen to the tissues, blood takes on a darker, bluish-red hue.

505: RBCs Have a Unique Shape

Red blood cells are shaped like flexible, biconcave discs. This unique shape increases their surface area for oxygen absorption and helps them squeeze through the tiniest blood vessels, called capillaries.

506: RBCs Lack a Nucleus

Unlike most cells in the body, red blood cells do not have a nucleus. This lack of a nucleus allows them to carry more hemoglobin and, consequently, more oxygen.

507: RBCs Are Produced in Bone Marrow

Red blood cells are made in the bone marrow through a process called erythropoiesis. The body produces about 2 million RBCs every second to replace old and damaged ones.

508: RBCs Have a Short Lifespan

Red blood cells have a lifetime of roughly 120 days. After this, they are broken down in the spleen and liver, and their components are recycled to produce new cells.

509: RBCs Travel 12,000 Miles Every Day

Over the course of their 120-day lifespan, red blood cells travel an estimated 12,000 miles (19,300 km) daily as they circulate through the body, delivering oxygen and picking up carbon dioxide.

510: Oxygen Delivery Is Critical for Cellular Function

Every cell in your body needs oxygen to perform basic functions, such as producing energy. Without red blood cells delivering oxygen, tissues would not be able to carry out vital processes, and organs would start to fail.

511: RBCs Also Remove Carbon Dioxide

In addition to delivering oxygen, red blood cells help remove carbon dioxide, a waste product produced by cells. They transport CO_2 to the lungs, where it is exhaled.

512: Iron Is Essential for Red Blood Cells

Iron is a key component of hemoglobin, and without enough iron, the body cannot produce healthy red blood cells. Iron-deficiency anemia occurs when the body lacks sufficient iron, leading to fatigue and weakness due to reduced oxygen transport.

513: The Spleen Filters Old RBCs

The spleen is commonly referred to as the "graveyard" of red blood cells. It filters out old or damaged RBCs and helps recycle their components, particularly iron, for the production of new red blood cells.

514: Blood Doping and RBCs

Athletes sometimes engage in blood doping—increasing their red blood cell count to enhance oxygen delivery and endurance. This is achieved by transfusing extra blood or using drugs that stimulate RBC production, though it is banned in professional sports.

515: Anemia Results from a Lack of RBCs

Anemia is a condition characterized by a deficiency in red blood cells or hemoglobin, leading to decreased oxygen delivery to tissues. It can result in fatigue, weakness, shortness of breath, and pale skin.

516: High Altitudes Increase RBC Production

When people live at high altitudes, where oxygen levels are lower, the body compensates by producing more red blood cells to carry enough oxygen. This natural adaptation improves oxygen transport and endurance over time.

517: Blood Transfusions Rely on RBCs

Blood transfusions are life-saving procedures in which patients receive red blood cells from donors. These transfusions are often used to treat anemia, blood loss, or certain medical conditions like sickle cell disease.

518: RBCs Carry Oxygen for a Vast Range of Activities

Whether you're sitting at rest or running a marathon, red blood cells adjust to deliver oxygen based on the body's needs. During exercise, for instance, RBCs increase the rate of oxygen delivery to meet the heightened demand of working muscles.

519: Blood Types Affect RBC Compatibility

Red blood cells have specific antigens on their surface that determine blood type (A, B, AB, or O). These antigens are important for blood transfusions, as receiving the wrong blood type can cause the immune system to attack the foreign red blood cells.

520: RBC Count Is a Key Health Indicator

Doctors often measure red blood cell count or hemoglobin levels in routine blood tests to assess overall health. Abnormal levels can indicate various health conditions, from dehydration to chronic diseases like kidney failure or leukemia.

521: The Body Recycles Red Blood Cells Efficiently

When red blood cells reach the end of their life cycle, the body efficiently recycles their components. Iron from hemoglobin is stored and used to create new RBCs, while other parts are converted into bilirubin and excreted in bile.

522: Some Animals Have Blue Blood

While humans and many animals have red blood due to hemoglobin, some animals, like horseshoe crabs and octopuses, have blue blood. This is because their blood contains hemocyanin, which uses copper instead of iron to bind oxygen.

WHITE BLOOD CELLS: THE BODY'S ARMY

523: White Blood Cells Protect You from Infections

White blood cells (WBCs), or leukocytes, are the body's first line of defense against infections. They identify, attack, and destroy harmful invaders like bacteria, viruses, fungi, and parasites.

524: Several Types of White Blood Cells

There are five main types of white blood cells, each with a specialized role:

525: Neutrophils: First responders that attack bacteria and fungi.

cells, which eliminate contaminated cells, and B cells, which generate antibodies, are examples of lymphocytes.
Monocytes: Turn into macrophages that engulf and digest pathogens.
Eosinophils: Involved in allergic responses and parasite attacks.
Lymphocytes: Include T cells, which kill infected cells, and B cells, which produce antibodies.

526: WBCs Are Made in Bone Marrow

Like red blood cells, white blood cells are produced in the bone marrow, the spongy tissue inside bones. They mature and enter the bloodstream to patrol for threats.

527: They Are Few in Number but Powerful

Although red blood cells outnumber white blood cells by about 700 to 1, WBCs are powerful enough to fight infections and keep the body healthy. In fact, the average adult has about 4,000 to 11,000 WBCs per microliter of blood.

528: WBCs Can Leave the Bloodstream

Unlike red blood cells, white blood cells can leave the bloodstream to move through tissues and attack pathogens where they're needed most. They can squeeze through the walls of blood vessels in a process called diapedesis.

529: WBCs Use Chemicals to Communicate

White blood cells communicate with each other and other cells using chemical signals called cytokines. These signals help coordinate the immune response, ensuring that the right cells are sent to fight the infection.

530: Phagocytes Eat Invaders

Some white blood cells, like neutrophils and macrophages, are phagocytes, meaning they engulf and digest harmful invaders through a process called phagocytosis. They literally "eat" the pathogen to neutralize it.

531: They Have Short Lives But Not All

Many white blood cells, like neutrophils, live for only a few hours or days while they fight off invaders. However, some, like memory T and B cells, can live for years, ensuring immunity against pathogens the body has encountered before.

532: WBCs Remember Past Infections

Memory cells, a type of lymphocyte, retain a "memory" of past infections. When the same pathogen invades the body again, these cells trigger a faster, more effective immune response, which is the principle behind vaccinations.

533: A High WBC Count Signals Infection

When your body detects an infection, it produces more white blood cells to fight it off. A high white blood cell count (leukocytosis) in a blood test often indicates that the body is battling an infection or inflammation.

534: Some White Blood Cells Release Toxins

Eosinophils and basophils release chemicals like histamine to fight parasites or to trigger inflammation during allergic reactions. In some cases, these responses can be harmful, such as in asthma or allergic reactions.

535: Autoimmune Diseases Involve WBC Malfunction

In autoimmune diseases, white blood cells mistakenly attack the body's own healthy cells, thinking they are foreign invaders. Diseases like rheumatoid arthritis, lupus, and multiple sclerosis are examples of this malfunction.

536: WBCs Are Critical in Allergic Reactions

During an allergic reaction, certain white blood cells, like basophils and eosinophils, overreact to harmless substances, such as pollen or dust, releasing chemicals like histamine, which causes symptoms like itching, sneezing, and swelling.

537: Leukemia Is a Cancer of White Blood Cells

One kind of malignancy that affects white blood cells is leukemia. It leads to the overproduction of abnormal WBCs, which can crowd out healthy cells and impair the immune system.

538: WBCs Help with Healing

White blood cells not only fight infections but also play a role in healing damaged tissues. Macrophages clean up debris from dead cells, and other WBCs release chemicals that promote the healing process.

539: HIV Targets White Blood Cells

The HIV virus specifically attacks and destroys CD4 T-cells, a type of lymphocyte, weakening the immune system. Without enough CD4 cells, the body becomes vulnerable to opportunistic infections and diseases.

540: WBCs Work in the Lymphatic System

In addition to patrolling the bloodstream, many white blood cells are part of the lymphatic system, which includes lymph nodes and lymphatic vessels. This system helps filter out pathogens and mount immune responses in localized areas.

541: Some WBCs Become "Natural Killer" Cells

Natural killer (NK) cells are a type of lymphocyte that can recognize and destroy cancer cells and virus-infected cells without needing to recognize specific antigens. They're part of the body's innate immune system.

542: Stress Affects WBCs

Chronic stress can weaken the immune system by affecting the production and function of white blood cells, making the body more susceptible to infections and illnesses. Maintaining a robust immune system requires effective stress management.

543: WBC Counts Can Be Measured Easily

A complete blood count (CBC) test measures the levels of different types of white blood cells in your blood. Doctors use this test to detect infections, immune disorders, and other medical conditions.

FUN FACTS ABOUT JOINTS

544: joints come in different types

Your body has several types of joints, including:

Hinge joints (like the elbow and rotational knee) that allow movement in one direction.
Ball-and-socket joints (like the hip and shoulder) that allow movement in many directions.
Pivot joints (like the neck) that allow movement.
Gliding joints (like in the wrists and ankles) that allow sliding motions.

545: There Are Over 230 Joints in the Human Body

The human body has 230 to 360 joints, depending on how you classify them, which enable a wide range of movements and flexibility, from bending your knees to swiveling your head.

546: Your Joints Are Surrounded by a Lubricant

Joints are surrounded by synovial fluid, a slippery substance that acts like natural lubrication, helping your joints move smoothly and reducing friction between bones during movement.

547: Knees Are the Largest Joints in Your Body

The biggest joint in the human body is the knee. It's a hinge joint that supports your body's weight and allows you to bend and straighten your legs. It's also one of the most complex and important joints for mobility.

548: Babies Have More Joints Than Adults

Babies are born with more joints than adults because many of their bones are not yet fused. Over time, certain bones grow together, reducing the number of joints as they age.

549: Cartilage Cushions Your Joints

The ends of bones in a joint are covered with a smooth, rubbery material called cartilage, which acts like a cushion, preventing bones from rubbing together and absorbing shock during movement.

550: Your Jaw Joint Is the Most Used Joint

The temporomandibular joint (TMJ), which connects your jaw to your skull, is the most frequently used joint in your body. Every time you talk, chew, yawn, or swallow, you're using this joint.

551: Cracking Your Knuckles Doesn't Cause Arthritis

Contrary to common assumption, arthritis is not caused by cracking your knuckles. The popping sound comes from bubbles in the synovial fluid in your joints. While it's harmless, it might annoy people around you!

552: Joints Can Be "Double-Jointed"

People who are double-jointed have hypermobile joints, meaning their ligaments and tendons are more elastic than average, allowing them to bend in ways that others can't. This trait is called joint hypermobility.

553: Shoulders Have the Greatest Range of Motion

Of all the joints in the body, the shoulder's ball-and-socket joint has the widest range of motion. It allows you to move your arm in nearly every direction: up, down, side-to-side, and around in circles.

554: Ligaments Keep Your Joints Together

Ligaments are tough bands of tissue that connect bones to each other within a joint, holding the joint in place and preventing it from moving too much in any direction, which keeps the bones stable.

555: Joints Become Stiffer with Age

As people age, their joints may become stiffer due to a loss of cartilage, a decrease in synovial fluid, or the development of conditions like osteoarthritis, which causes joint pain and inflammation.

556: The Hip Joint Is One of the Strongest Joints

Your hip joint is a powerful ball-and-socket joint that bears a lot of your body's weight. It's designed for both stability and flexibility, making it essential for activities like walking, running, and jumping.

557: You Can Strengthen Your Joints Through Exercise

Regular exercise helps maintain joint flexibility and strength. Activities like swimming, yoga, and walking can strengthen the muscles around joints, supporting their function and reducing the risk of injury.

558: Joint Replacement Surgery Is Common

Joint replacement surgeries, like hip or knee replacements, are increasingly common, especially among older adults. These surgeries involve replacing damaged joints with prosthetic implants, restoring movement and reducing pain.

559: Your Ankles Are Surprisingly Flexible

The ankle joint allows for a wide range of movement, including flexion, extension, and slight rotation. Despite being small, ankles can withstand a lot of pressure, especially during activities like running and jumping.

560: Some Joints Don't Move

Not all joints are mobile. Fibrous joints, like those in the skull, are fixed and don't allow movement. These joints help protect vital organs, like the brain, by keeping the bones securely fused together.

561: Cartilage Can't Heal Itself Easily

Unlike bones, which can repair themselves after a fracture, cartilage has no blood supply, making it difficult to heal once damaged. This is why injuries like a torn meniscus in the knee often require medical treatment.

562: Your Spine Is Made of Multiple Joints

The spine consists of a series of vertebrae connected by facet joints, which allow for flexibility and movement while protecting the spinal cord. These joints enable you to bend, twist, and stand upright.

563: Arthritis Affects Millions of People Worldwide

Arthritis is a common joint disorder that affects millions of people worldwide, causing pain, swelling, and stiffness in joints. Osteoarthritis is the most common form, often linked to aging and joint wear and tear.

564: Hydration Helps Your Joints

Staying hydrated is important for maintaining healthy joints. The majority of synovial fluid, which lubricates your joints, is composed of water. Drinking plenty of water can help keep your joints moving smoothly.

565: Finger Joints Are Small but Complex

The joints in your fingers are some of the smallest and most intricate joints in your body, allowing for fine motor skills like gripping, writing, and typing. They are hinge joints that enable bending and straightening.

566: Your Elbow Is a Hinge Joint

The elbow functions as a hinge joint, but it also allows for rotation of the forearm, thanks to the way the radius and ulna bones connect to the humerus. This combination gives your arm flexibility and precision.

567: Running on Hard Surfaces Can Stress Your Joints

Running on hard surfaces like concrete can increase the impact on your joints, especially the knees, hips, and ankles. To protect your joints, it's recommended to run on softer surfaces like grass or dirt when possible.

568: Flexibility Can Decrease Joint Pain

Maintaining good flexibility can help reduce joint pain by keeping the muscles and tendons around the joints loose and healthy. Stretching exercises and activities like yoga can enhance flexibility and joint range of motion.

CONCLUSION

The human body is an extraordinary machine, intricately designed with a remarkable balance of strength, flexibility, and complexity. From the framework of your bones and the power of your muscles to the defense mechanisms of your immune system, every part plays a vital role in maintaining life and health. These fascinating facts about the human body from the wonders of the skin, heart, and brain to the intricacies of organs and systems highlight how each element works in harmony, ensuring you can move, think, breathe, and grow.

By understanding and appreciating these incredible facts, you can better care for your body and marvel at the amazing biological systems that sustain you every day. Whether it's through exercise, nutrition, or mindfulness, maintaining a healthy balance is key to ensuring that your body continues to function optimally, supporting your journey through life. So next time you take a breath, stretch a muscle, or feel your heart race, remember how truly amazing your body is!